COMPUTE!'s
COMPUTER SECURITY

Ralph Roberts
and
Pamela Kane

COMPUTE! Books
Greensboro, North Carolina
Radnor, Pennsylvania

Printed in the United States of America

10 9 8 7 6 5 4 3 2 1

ISBN 0-87455-188-9

Library of Congress Catalog Card Number 88-63151

COMPUTE! Books, Post Office Box 5406, Greensboro, NC 27403, (919) 275-9809, is a Capital Cities/ABC, Inc. company and is not associated with any manufacturer of personal computers. IBM is a registered trademark and OS/2 is a trademark of International Business Machines Corporation. MS-DOS is a registered trademark of Microsoft Corporation. Apple and Macintosh are trademarks of Apple Computer, Inc. Guard Card is a registered trademark of NorthBank Corporation. Disk Defender is a registered trademark of Director Technologies, Inc.

CONTENTS

Preface .... *v*
Acknowledgments .... *vii*

1. Like Thieves in the Night 1
2. This Is a Stickup, Press Enter to Continue 9
3. Technical Limitations 25
4. Physical Security 37
5. Data Security 57
6. Security Overview 67
   Chuck Gilmore
7. Computer Viruses 75
8. Thieves in Three-Piece Suits 83
9. Communication and Network Security 95
10. Encryption and Passwords 109
11. Security Planning 121
12. IBM PCs and Clones 137
13. OS/2 149
    Chuck Gilmore
14. Macintosh 153
15. Stand by to Repel Boarders 157

Index 167

PREFACE

We live in the Information Age. Data is our currency. Computers hold our fortunes. The changes in all of our lives made by computers continue to grow as data processing in general and the personal computer in specific permeate and define our day-to-day existence. There is no escape.

Walk through the checkout line in your local supermarket and the new electronic cash registers beep greedily as they scan bar codes on the packages of food you buy and tally up astonishing totals. Stop by the bank to replenish your cash, and an Automatic Teller Machine (ATM) asks for a taste of your plastic. In the workplace, pursuing entertainment, and in our very homes—computers are everywhere.

We sometimes lose sight of just what computers really are—simply appliances to help us manipulate information faster. Not only are the appliances valuable, but the information they contain may be priceless. Computer security specialists and this book are concerned with the physical security of equipment and the protection of these significant financial investments, but even more emphasis must be placed on *data security*. If someone steals $3,000 worth of computer hardware, including a 20 megabyte hard disk and/or some floppy disks, your insurance company will probably come forth with a check for the replacement value. But what about the data on that hard disk or those floppies that disappeared?

An equipment theft that appears to be simple could allow a thief to go on stealing from you for days, weeks, months, or even years! Your credit card numbers, your checking and savings account information, proprietary company secrets such as customer lists—all these and much more can be used to advantage by technically oriented thieves.

Knowledge is power. In this case, it could be power over you.

It's not even necessary for a thief to actually take the equipment. If he or she merely copies the *information*, it might be too late before you discover your own data being used against you or your company. Nor need the thief be active or malicious. An interruption in electrical supply, a child, a cat or a co-worker tripping over an essential cable, a disk with your Great American Novel used as a coaster or a frisbee—you can also steal from yourself.

In this age also of electronic terrorism, you not only have to worry about thieves, but also *computer viruses* and hackers gaining access to your system—destroying, or worse, altering data to their own warped ends. This book deals with these very real threats also.

Whether you're a single computer owner or the manager of a large area network for a business, a school, or any other user of computers, *COMPUTE!'s Computer Security* offers relief from the fear and the very real danger of violations to your system. It will help you understand and implement ways to protect yourself from simple physical theft or damage of hardware to the potentially much more devastating stealing or destruction of information.

The authors are both well-versed in computer security. They offer you not only the advantage of their long experience, but also that of many other experts contacted during the research of this book. And it's all written in an enjoyable, jargon-free manner that everyone can understand. So, now—on to safe computing. Knowledge is power!

Acknowledgments

Thanks to Glenn Bleakney, Paul Cottrell, Jon David, Jan Diamondstone, Barbara Hines, Ross Greenberg, Chuck Gilmore, Donn Parker, Mike Reimer, Sandy Sherizan, Dick tenEyck, and Ken Weiss for their help, whether by written words, shared insights, or my observations.

A somewhat backhanded thanks to those who have shown, by bad example, what is wrong with this industry and provided so many horror stories to use as teaching examples. They shall remain nameless.

Special thanks to my coauthor and wonderful friend, Ralph Roberts, who has been a model of patience and professionalism to a first-time author. Thanks also to COMPUTE! Books, especially to Stephen Levy for joining Ralph in seeing more in me than I could imagine. The last and best thanks go to my family: To Lizzie, J.T., Max, and Rob for waiting for dinner (and the computer) until the next chapter was done. To my parents who have waited patiently through so much. (Hi, Mom!) And, almost beyond words, thanks to Andy who has truly been "the wind beneath my wings."

—Pam Kane

1
LIKE THIEVES
IN THE NIGHT

How old is crime? Far older than computers, that's for sure.
One of the first cavewomen, so goes a certain legend, amassed
a large collection of beautifully colored stones through hard and
diligent effort. The stones' glitter and pleasing textures were her
pride and joy. On a dark night, someone broke into her cave
and took them all.

Soon afterwards the disgusted cavepeople, who were now
suffering from a rash of cave burglaries and mammoth rustling,
started the world's first law enforcement agency. A nearby tribe
whose experience with theft was greater, offered advice for a fee
and started the world's first security consulting business.

More seriously, stealing is an unfortunate human aberra-
tion that has troubled all generations throughout history. It is
at least as old as humanity. Ancient kings built great castles not
so much to keep their enemies out as their gold *in.*

Crime is still very much a part of our everyday lives, as
are certain basic security precautions. Society—through the medium of local, state, and federal government—tries to antici-
pate and protect us from the criminal bent of our fellow
citizens. Not only are there police and other law enforcement
agencies, but regulatory ones as well to make sure our food is
pure and our cars have seat belts.

As our society evolves, so does the criminal mind and the
available methods.

A disgruntled insurance company employee in Texas was
recently convicted of concocting what the popular press has
termed as a computer virus that destroyed 168,000 payroll
records (it was actually a "worm" instead of a virus, but more
about that later). This company learned the hard way about

1

one of the three major areas of computer security, *data security*. The others are *physical security*, which includes both the actual safeguarding of computer equipment and the prevention of its misuse, and *communications security*. These three areas are often interdependent.

If your laptop computer is stolen on the subway, not only is the actual hardware investment lost, but so too is the data inside. Should a salesperson from a rival firm be surreptitiously looking over your shoulder while you use that laptop to do a spreadsheet of monthly sales, that too is thievery because your proprietary information has been compromised.

Information—Today's Gold

The ultimate responsibility for protection of yourself and your property rests with *you*. Lock your doors at night, don't leave money lying on the counter in the store, and never walk down a dark alley alone. If what you have is at all valuable, some light-fingered character will purloin it if given an instant's opportunity. This is a simple and universal reality.

Fifty centuries and more of recorded human history have prepared us for physical theft. Coming into a burglarized office or home is a shock and a personal violation of our own space, but we *understand* this type of ripoff on both a conscious and subconscious level. We know that tangible valuables, if not adequately protected, are subject to thieves. No matter where we live, the 11 o'clock news is full of crime reports lest we forget.

Harder to immediately comprehend and grasp are the sometimes awesome levels of damaging ramifications caused by the theft of *information*. On a conscious level we realize this is now the Information Age, and computers allow us to manipulate vast amounts of data. Most of us, even those of us who make our living disseminating information, don't have the same protective instincts for such an abstract thing as data as we do for physical valuables. We would *never* leave a wallet or purse lying on the desk in an office open to the public, yet we leave computers or computer terminals turned on, with important information on the screens.

A potential thief merely has to stroll over and look at an active screen. Given enough time, he or she could scroll though your company's confidential data, or even make a quick copy and conceal the floppy within the pages of a newspaper or magazine.

Here's an example. One of the authors of this book, having recently purchased a streaming tape backup for his hundred megabytes of hard disks, decided to get a safety deposit box. His information on the resulting tapes includes several books and the extensive databases that provided research material for the books. His very livelihood was contained in the material on those tapes, and he wanted to make sure a copy always existed in a separate, secure location in case of burglary, equipment malfunction, fire, or any other catastrophe that could wipe out the information in his home office.

Getting the safety deposit box was no problem for him. It might have been for the bank, since he had arrived at noon, and several of the bank's people were gone to lunch. He was told to have a seat and someone would be with him momentarily. Instead, he roamed about the offices, amusing himself by reading all the computer screens left on at empty desks. He made a mental note to use the experience as an example in this book. Would you want a stranger reading your checking account balance? It was relatively easy to look at both the tellers' and loan screens and no one noticed, cared, or asked him to sit back down. If a *bank* is this lax about computer security, what about other businesses?

Information is *gold* in this new age. We have to understand this and protect it just as we would precious metal or stones. And computer media—hard disks, floppy disks, and backup tapes—are now the repositories of this "gold." If your personal or business financial data is in a computer, think of that computer as a safe and don't leave the door open when you're away.

Deliberate Data Destruction

Valuable information, of course, is far more than just financial records. We've already mentioned customer lists, and here's a recent example of how a company and its employees got burned through the loss of another type of information—payroll records.

As we mentioned earlier, a disgruntled former employee of a Texas insurance company wreaked havoc on his ex-employer. As reported by the Associated Press on September 20, 1988, he paid for his vindictive act by becoming the first person believed to have been convicted of planting a computer virus. In fact, the planted program was not a virus, but rather a "worm" coupled with a "Trojan horse." Both viruses and worms have the common attribute of being small computer programs often hidden in apparently normal software. The program causes a computer to modify or erase data at a given time or when a certain sequence of commands is seen by the system (the difference between them being that a virus can replicate itself and infect other programs). In this case, the damage occurred two days after the employee was dismissed.

The ex-employee of the insurance company, a 40-year-old computer programmer named Donald Gene Burleson, was charged with destroying 168,000 payroll records. His actual conviction was for "harmful access to a computer," which is a third-degree felony (reflecting the Law's creaky but growing concern about information-related crimes). A Tarrant County (Texas) jury deliberated for six hours and found him guilty as charged. He faces a possible sentence of as much as ten years in prison and a $5,000 fine.

"As far as I know, it's the first case of this type in the nation," said Davis McCown, an assistant district attorney quoted in the AP news story. "We've had people stealing through computers, but not this." He added, "There was a series of programs built into the system as early as Labor Day of 1985."

The jury was told during the trial that the ex-employee had planted a virus in the computer system of his employer, the USPA, and IRA company, which is a Fort Worth–based insurance and brokerage firm. While most companies try to hide their lapses of computer security, this one became a matter of public record through the trial and news reports. Assistant DA McCown told the jury that Burleson had constructed the program to act like a time bomb. The program activated itself on September 21, 1985, two days after Mr. Burleson was dismissed from his job as a programmer. "Once he got fired, those programs went off," Mr. McCowan said. The company stated that

4

Burleson had personality conflicts with other employees. Despite the virus being discovered only two days later, it had already eliminated 168,000 payroll records. Paychecks to company employees were held up for more than a month.

Burleson's defense lawyers said during the trial that he was a victim of a scheme by someone else who had used his terminal and access code. Although this was disproved during the trial, it makes an important point. If you have access to a system, be it a company network or even one of the commercial ones like Delphi, Summit, or Compuserve, guard your password well. You could wind up not just losing a lot of money, but accused of a crime you didn't commit.

Burleson also lost a civil case brought against him by USPA in connection with the incident. The jury in that case, as reported by the Associated Press, ordered him to pay his former employers $12,000.

With stories like this, people are beginning to take computer crime very seriously. It's truly unfortunate that books like this one are necessary to help us all protect ourselves and our property, but *fortunate* that the increased awareness may prevent further losses.

Slime Rises to the Top

Fear is a great motivator. Visceral reactions ("fight or flight") can shut down conscious thought processes. Lack of knowledge feeds fear.

The history of Man abounds with stories of trading on fear. These include such things as the "indulgences" sold by the Church in the Middle Ages, the charms and talismans of the tribal shaman to ward off evil spirits, lotions and potions to prevent the aging process or restore lost youth, and miracle "cures" for cancer.

The "techno-fear" of the late 1980s has become computer security. Otherwise normal, rational people—people whose education and skill levels allow them to operate highly sophisticated computers—suddenly see lurking viruses on every disk, on every bulletin board. But, of course, our high priests of knowledge—the press—have told us it's true. And those who stand to profit from our fear swear to it.

Just as the snake-oil salesman with the traveling show probably made more money in one night than the hometown physician made in a year, vendors of "miracle" software hope to pile up the megabucks and get out of town fast before it's discovered that a Band-Aid is no substitute for long-term care.

There is a software product currently being marketed as a virus killer: "100 percent effective against all viruses!" screams the product's literature. Unfortunately, it's also 100 percent effective against some standard utilities. This is what happened:

The miracle product was purchased and loaded into a programmer's PC for a standard staff evaluation. As a TSR (Terminate and Stay Resident) utility, it camped out in its chosen location in RAM (Random Access Memory) and was more or less invisible *until* . . . .

The programmer, trying to remember exactly how a previous section of code had been written, called up her current file in a "window" on the bottom half of the screen. She found what she needed to know and pressed the function key to restore the full screen. The commercial utility and the miracle cure both required the same area of RAM and went to war over the territory.

Who won? Nobody. Who lost? The programmer. Over 4,000 lines of program code were reduced to a screenful of garbage.

Luckily the programmer possessed three important attributes—a sense of humor, a sense of responsibility, and a good current backup. Portions of her memo on the "undocumented features" of the miracle software contained some sections inappropriate for publication, but little time was lost and the "cure" consigned to the snake-oil file of a company with over 20,000 PCs. Appropriate memoranda flew from the MIS people to all PC Coordinators and users over speedy electronic mail.

Another facet of the human condition in this technical age is that many of us don't like to admit there's something we might not know. We tend to nod sagely when someone whose technical competence seems to be superior states, "The ABC when connected by a DEF to the HIJ will output the KLM to OPR." You bet.

There is, however, no disgrace in being "underknowledged," as a favorite 11-year-old says, in a world where development time and changes are measured in nanoseconds. But, while ignorance may be bliss, it's no excuse either.

Greed

Once upon a time, the "computer consultant" was the absolute source of all knowledge—especially for smaller entities without in-house resources. Companies wishing to position themselves on the technical leading edge became unwitting victims for unscrupulous salespeople who had adopted the title "consultant."

A particularly memorable example, well documented in a large number of legal proceedings, is that of a salesperson who was fired by his giant corporate employer for selling "vaporware" to clients and misrepresenting the products he was being paid to sell.

Undaunted, he went out and set up his own business. Knowing well what the marketplace wanted, he proceeded to sell to its needs and desires. Never mind that the products did not exist. He soon discovered the additional profits available from creating software/hardware dependencies.

"If you want this product," he would tell prospective clients, "you will have to purchase this system, which we will sell to you at the best possible price."

With a gift of "baffle gab," swift movement, and constantly shifting priorities and sales techniques, he stayed ahead of the process server for a long time—to the detriment of his customers. Later, we'll tell you how to detect this kind of technical ripoff and what you can do about it.

What is Computer Security?

At the beginning of this chapter you met the three major forms of computer security. They are *data security, physical security* (which, again, includes both the actual safeguarding of computer equipment and the prevention of its misuse) and *communications security.*

Data security is the most important concept related to the whole field of computer security. Once more we emphasize that information is *valuable,* and this fact is something we humans don't instinctively realize. Thus, information integrity is far too often treated thoughtlessly or cavalierly. In effect, it's left "lying around" for any thief who happens along.

If you get nothing more out of this book than a sense of just how important and valuable information is, then you will have gained a great deal. Information is money! Knowledge is power! Data is precious!

While we cover the other aspects of computer security in these pages, the main thrust is how you can protect your *information*. Encryption, limiting access, passwords—these are just a few of the techniques we'll discuss.

Nor is data security limited to just guarding against criminal acts. The very vulnerability and delicacy of computers themselves (something computer manufacturers and computer sales people like to gloss over) means there are many ways your data can disappear. We'll cover good backup procedure and the other ways to safeguard against this type of loss and loss from viruses, Trojans, logic bombs, and similar afflictions now besetting the computing community.

Physical security will find all of us on more familiar ground. This includes protecting against the actual theft of your hardware, but in some special ways unique to the world of computers.

Communications security is somewhat of a gray area in that it overlaps both data and physical security—having elements of each. If you or your company are moving data over the phone lines, opportunities for its pilfering obviously exist. We'll talk about how to minimize your risks and how to prevent hackers and others from gaining access to your system via telephones.

2
THIS IS A STICKUP, PRESS ENTER TO CONTINUE

Bonnie and Clyde never had it so good. The average bank robber today may get a few thousand, but the typical white-collar computer criminal can easily collect hundreds of thousands or even *millions* of dollars and go undetected for months or years. And, while bank robbers often get shot at, computer criminals are seldom even seen.

Such concepts as "Salami" techniques, "superzapping," and "trapdoors" are examples of the ways and means of computer crime. This chapter gives a brief historical view of such crime, and explains these techniques and others. It gives you an insight into computer crime and computer criminals that will help you throughout this book.

The History of Computer Crime

With the widespread computerization of large companies in the 1960s, computer crime grew and blossomed. As necessary as computers were to the success of big business, the only ones who understood these new controllers of information were programmers; a company was often at the mercy of a less than honest programmer. In the 1970s, as the minicomputer came down in price, more and more companies saw them as cost effective tools. Both the number of machines in use and the opportunity for and incidence of computer crime went up dramatically.

The 1980s welcomed the newest, least expensive, and easiest to use computer yet—the PC (microcomputer). Computer ownership and use has increased by literally *millions* of systems. There are now computers in homes, in offices, and in schools all over the world. Obviously, the opportunities for a prospective computer criminal have gone up by many orders of magnitude and anyone who can find the red switch and read a book may fall into the way of temptation. Even the smallest companies must now be automated in order to compete and survive in today's business environment. Even the youngest children are taught computer skills in school. The opportunity window for those with a larcenous bent grows day by day.

Computer crime in the past was made easier for technically oriented white-collar criminals because most employers and managers simply didn't understand what was really involved. Fearful of appearing undereducated or not in control, management simply abrogated responsibility to those in the computer room.

Donn B. Parker—now a senior management systems consultant with SRI in Menlo Park, California—relates a somewhat amusing example of this in his own book *Crime By Computer* (Charles Scribner's Sons, 1976). The story goes something like this:

In 1971, far before the personal computer age, a small accounting company hired a brilliant young programmer to set them up on one of those "newfangled" computers. The programmer wrote a series of programs that did the job excellently. The company became totally dependent on him and his system.

chance to make a quick killing. He gathered up all the programs and went off to hide in the mountains. After allowing time for his employer to panic and the pressure from equally panicked clients to build, he called the employer and demanded $100,000 ransom to return the programs.

Unfortunately for the programmer, his skills did not extend to extortion. The local sheriff located him within three days, placed the young man under arrest for grand theft, and seized the computer programs as evidence. The sheriff proceeded to lock all the programming material in his evidence room and sat back smugly to await the trial. While the wheels of Justice were grinding exceedingly slow (as they usually do), trial was scheduled for several weeks after the arrest.

Here's when the whole thing started to become more like a Hollywood film than real life. The small company, relieved that their all-important programs had been rescued, asked for them back. The sheriff's people were uncooperative and not at all sure what a computer program was anyway. The programs were evidence and *no* one was going to touch them until *after* the trial.

The accounting firm was just about out of business. Heroic measures were required. In desperation, the president of the company *broke* into the sheriff's office and retrieved his programs. He took them to a data center, had copies made, then broke *back* into the sheriff's office to return the originals. His luck was exceptional, if not his judgment, and he got away with it—saving his company.

But the story doesn't end there. When the preliminary hearing was held, the prosecutor shared the sheriff's confusion and lack of knowledge about computers. He decided it would not be possible to get a conviction due to the lack of legal precedent concerning computer programs being used in extortion. So the end result was that the young programmer walked away scot-free while the president of the accounting firm had been put to a lot of trouble, anguish, and legal expense, not to mention the risk of jail if he'd been caught red-handed stealing back his own property.

Ripping Off Ma Bell for Fun and Profit

The above computer crime was unsuccessful, but Parker also tells of another computer criminal who stole perhaps hundreds of thousands of dollars worth of equipment from Pacific Bell back in the early 1970s. The resulting arrest and trial was covered in the popular press at the time and caused a lot of excitement because of its scope and the ingenuity of the perpetrator.

Far greater detail is contained in *Crime By Computer* (and we recommend that book to you for not only this story, but

11

many other fascinating ones as well). Here's a brief synopsis of this computer caper:

Jerry Schneider was a bright young man who already had his own company to market his electronic inventions when he was a student in a Los Angeles area high school in 1968. On his way to and from school everyday he passed a Pacific Telephone and Telegraph Company supply office (at that time, Pacific was still part of AT&T).

Like many other technically inclined youngsters growing up in the 1960s, Jerry was unable to pass a trash bin of an electronics company without investigation (such as the coauthor of this book, who was a ham radio operator, and found tons of great parts that way—*free* being an affordable price!). Nothing wrong with scrounging; the stuff was being dumped anyway, and Jerry found many parts and equipment he could salvage for his own use.

However, there were also papers mixed in with the good stuff in the trash. Such important intelligence as *Bell System Guides to Ordering Parts, Computer Program Listings,* and much more. Unknowingly, Pacific Telephone was spewing out its guts and leading Jerry Schneider into temptation.

Before long, Jerry had carefully sorted out a complete set of Pacific's proprietary documents, put them in ring binders, and this high school kid now knew as much about the supply office's operations as the employees. He also retrieved bills of lading, invoices, various company memos, and (an important item) budget listings.

After high school, Jerry went to college and expanded his business in his spare time. He used his knowledge of telephone equipment (and the scrounged parts) to sell refurbished Western Electric equipment. Western Electric was at that time the wholly owned manufacturing arm of AT&T. So far, he was doing nothing wrong and, in fact, showing a great deal of laudable creative initiative. But Jerry wanted success a little too quickly and decided the telephone company could help him get it— without them even realizing it.

To finish out his already comprehensive knowledge of their operations, he posed as a freelance writer and visited various company installations. He enjoyed the phone company's courtesy during a number of presentations and tours of telephone facilities. As with the trash, the phone company continued to innocently divulge secrets.

Jerry then did a lot of careful planning. He moved his business to a larger location and then bought an old telephone company van at one of its own auctions. The van still had the phone company logos on its sides. He also managed to obtain keys to the supply facility gates by the ruse of representing himself as an employee (he used a recent employee's name) and saying he had lost his keys.

Now comes the computer part. Pacific was using a computerized inventory ordering system based on an IBM 360 computer. Orders for equipment were sent in on punched cards, which were then fed into the computer. Knowing the budgets for each location and having figured out a way in which theft would be "invisible" to the phone company's inventory, Jerry was ready to start ordering for himself.

His first order, placed into the phone company's system in late June of 1971 was for over $30,000 worth of equipment! The order was delivered to the supply office one night and Jerry simply drove to the loading dock early the next morning and loaded it into his "company" truck.

He did this almost *every day* for *the next seven months*.

The ability to order genuine telephone company equipment at a great price—free—enabled his company to grow rapidly (he marked the stolen equipment with an official looking stamp reading "Released for Resale"). He soon had ten employees. Customers were astounded at how quickly he could fill their highly specialized orders.

This might have gone on for a long time, but Jerry was trying to do too much at once. In addition to his early morning trips to pick up telephone equipment, he was going to night school and running his business. He decided to bring one of his employees into the scheme.

The accomplice soon wanted more money. Jerry refused and fired him. The miffed ex-employee turned Schneider in to Pacific Telephone and Telegraph. The phone company was less than impressed that it was subsidizing someone else's business, and Jerry not only wound up in jail but was a defendant in a civil suit against him.

The sensational headlines in various papers at the time included "How to Steal a Million from a Computer," "Computer Accomplice in Theft," and (our favorite) "How He Folded, Spindled, and Mutilated." Since the telephone company was anxious to downplay this now-classic computer crime, it claimed that only $65,000 or so was lost. Jerry himself said it was more like $800,000 to $900,000. But, at $30,000 every business day for over seven months, the total take could have easily been in the millions.

Jerry Schneider was convicted and served time for his crime. He also lost the civil suit brought by the phone company and had to pay them several thousand dollars. Upon his release, he went "straight" and founded a computer security consulting business to help other companies avoid computer crime on the basis of "it takes a thief to catch a thief." He got plenty of clients except, not surprisingly, AT&T and Pacific Telephone. Both declined his services, probably not wanting to contribute to his success a second time.

Computer Crime—Anyone Can Do it Now

There are two basic types of computer security violations— those done by insiders and those perpetrated by outsiders. Let's look at the latter first, since this is the kind that usually makes the AP wires and nightly news reports.

One of the most recent computer crimes involves an 18-year-old Chicagoan. According to Charles Bowen, writing in the October 1988 issue of *Live Wire* (the monthly publication of the GEnie computer network), Herbert Zinn of Chicago has been charged with breaking into various computer systems. These installations include those of AT&T (a perennial favorite of computer criminals) and of *NATO* (the North Atlantic Treaty Organization)! The charges against Zinn include the theft of software worth more than a million dollars.

Zinn apparently also made a generous attempt to share his wealth with fellow hackers. He was accused of leaving messages on a computer bulletin board system in Texas called "Phreak Class-2600" (the term *phreak* is one used by hackers to mean circumventing security procedures and gaining access to systems over the *phone*). The messages told readers how they, too, could circumvent AT&T's security devices and protocols. An "underground" magazine, also called *2600*, routinely publishes instructions and information for phone phreaking, though *2600's* main focus has recently turned to computers rather than phones. One recent issue was dedicated almost entirely to the "virus" issue.

Unlike the example of Jerry Schneider in the early 1970s, who had to accomplish his theft by physically turning in punched cards, today's computer criminals can simply call their victim's computer system on the phone or a fax machine.

Consumertronics (P.O. Drawer 537, Alamogordo, NM 88310) offers a series of booklets on various aspects of security and "computer phreaking" (list available on request). In *Computer Phreaking Addendum* ("sold for educational purposes only"), author John J. Williams discusses how to "phreak" computer systems, and also how computer viruses work. Mr. Williams offers several examples of computer crimes, extracted from various wire service reports (you can buy booklets on numerous other computer security related subjects as well; write the above address for a list).

In July 1987, for example, nine teenagers in Pittsburgh were arrested and charged with computer fraud. They used stolen credit card numbers to make thousands of dollars in purchases. The numbers were obtained when they used their personal computers to raid the files of a credit card authorization service on the West Coast. The service kindly gave them a lengthy list of valid card numbers and expiration dates.

Another group of teenagers, this one in New Jersey, obtained and listed on various computer bulletin boards such things as the private phone numbers of high-ranking Pentagon officers, credit card numbers, and plans for building bombs. They were charged with computer fraud and conspiracy. Their computer equipment and disks were confiscated by the police.

In New Mexico, an incident involved the son of an employee of the White Sands Missile Range. He published an official AT&T phone credit card number on a hacker's BBS. Over $10,000 in long distance calls were made by various people before this was discovered. Both the boy and his father are now in the process of making good the charges.

We are not knocking young people here. While there is a strong hacker subculture consisting mostly of young men (young women apparently don't go in for hacking) in their teens and early twenties, they are responsible for only a small portion of all computer crime. The fact that they're young and achieving feats that are almost unimaginable to the general public assures the press will play up such incidents whenever they come to light. The winner of the national spelling bee is always on the *Johnny Carson Show*. And a kid who flies his dad's plane across the country is on all the talk shows. Kids who spray paint "LEX41" on the IRT are lionized as important contemporary artists.

The *reason* that kids can get into highly sensitive and sophisticated systems is traceable to a lack of proper system security procedures. They do it because it's easy.

Hackers and Phreakers

During the 1960s when *hacker* was a term of respect, young people at such places as the Massachusetts Institute of Technology were doing things with computers that had never been done before. These included wondrous and glorious things like inventing the game Space War and sitting up all night coding the most elegant "hack" (program) possible, subsisting on candy bars and soft drinks. Out of this group came many of the people who first conceived of personal computing, then made it possible despite all the nay saying of the "big machine" people. We owe them a great debt.

One honorable pursuit in this infancy of personal interaction with computers was to play with the mind of your friends by messing up their program code. You won points and respect by introducing a problem that would be undetectable for as long as possible. Watching the friend go crazy as the program bombed time after time for inexplicable reasons was considered great sport.

These clandestine modifications to code were not viruses; they were *bombs* (taking immediate effect). Yet, these bombs proved that controlling another person's program to your own ends was possible. The perhaps one universal rule of all mankind is that if something is possible, someone, somewhere, for some reason (sane or not) will do it. We can then attach the addendum that others will hear of this thing being done and do it themselves.

As we saw in the preceding section, there is now a subculture of young people who break into computers for a variety of reasons, ranging from just on a lark to out and out larceny. The press calls them "hackers." They describe themselves as "phreakers," and that is a better term to use instead of sullying the honor that true hackers have achieved.

To give them credit where credit is due, these kids are certainly on the leading edge of computing. If nothing else, they serve as an example of just how poor general security is on many large systems.

Let's go back to our friend Pacific Bell again. Recently, as reported in the August 1, 1988 *Business Week*, they were the target of a group of teenage phreakers. The youngsters pulled a simple con game on telephone employees. They would call up legitimate employees and convince them to divulge computer passwords.

"Hey, I forgot the password, and this work has to go in. Can you help me out?"

It worked great. Once the phreakers got into the phone company computers, they would then modify work orders, cause disruptions in service, and do various other malicious acts.

The same article in *Business Week* (the cover feature, "Is Your Computer Secure?") quotes Gerald E. Mitchell, who's in charge of data security for IDS Financial Services, as saying since there are now 33 million desktop computers in use, several hundred thousand people now have learned the technical skills needed to "penetrate most systems."

Here are a few horrifying examples. A group of West German phreakers (part of the infamous "Chaos Computer Club" in Hamburg) used the international phone lines to make repeated accesses of NASA computers in 1987, as well as a number of U.S. military networks. It took three months of work (and a lot of *our* tax dollars) for NASA to change passwords

17

and to remove "trap door" programs left by the Germans.

Another German phreaker spent almost *two years* looking at U.S. Defense Department data by calling computers in the United States from Germany before he was finally caught (phreakers don't worry about long distance charges because they circumvent those too). In another incident, an unidentified phreaker broke into the computers at NASA's Jet Propulsion Laboratory in Pasadena, California.

We could go on with horror story after horror story, but you should have the idea by now. Computer security is important.

Betrayal of Trust

But, as scary as phreakers may be, the real and most dangerous long-term computer thieves are usually vipers within the bosom of a company—trusted employees. People working for a corporation have greater access to its secrets and a far greater opportunity to misuse its computers than any outsider. These are the crimes we hear least about, since a company doesn't want to lose the public's trust or its own stature in the industry by admitting it lost a million dollars to one of its own employees or that thousands of customer records have been destroyed.

While nonprogrammers can and do steal, those with programming knowledge and access can rack up the biggest scores. A recent government publication, *Criminal Justice Manual: Computer Crime*, defined some of the methods used:

Logic Bombs. A logic bomb is a computer program secretly installed in a system and designed to perform a certain defined action. The program carries out this action when the conditions embedded within it have been satisfied. A logic bomb may be activated upon completion of a specific period of elapsed time, by another program being run a number of times, or on a certain time and date. The result may be destroyed or altered files, or something more subtle such as amounts of money, inventory, or data being transferred to a place where the criminal can access it.

Some of the techniques that have been used to defraud or destroy by computer from the late 1950s are also used in the sick world of those who hatch and unleash computer viruses today. A *logic bomb* is one of these. This is a clandestine portion of a program that's executed when the computer determines that certain conditions have been met. These conditions can be satisfied by elapsed time, the number of times the program has run, or, more commonly, on a certain date.

There have been numerous instances where a programmer who quit or was fired from a large company left such a bomb in the system. These logic bombs have done such things as simply shut down the system on the programmer's birthday, in effect taking the day off, to maliciously destroying thousands of important records. Again, if it can be done (and it certainly *can*), someone will do it.

Salami Techniques. Salami Techniques are routines written into programs that take a small "slice" of assets from a large number of accounts, thus making their detection difficult. First, the overall amounts are small, and even smaller still for each individual account. This type of fraud actually existed long before computers and is also known as the "round down" technique. As an example, if all the odd change amounts (or even just part of them) were diverted during the course of a bank's normal monthly business, the money can really mount up for the criminal. Maybe only eight or nine cents per transaction goes into his "personal" account, but after a million transactions at computer speed, that could easily be 80 or 90 thousand dollars!

Superzapping. Superzapping is the technique used by utility programs that most large computer centers employ during program development. This utility will bypass all security and other controls whenever the programmer needs to get into the computer to fix a bug, such as the computer locking up due to a program gone wild. It's analogous to a master key a hotel detective carries that will unlock every room in a hotel. All a computer criminal would need is a copy of this program for the target system or—even scarier—authorized system access.

Trap Doors. Programs developed for large computer systems, such as those used by giant banks and corporations, usually won't allow extra lines to be inserted into the program. Naturally, programmers must have a way of making changes during the development process, and for putting in improvements later. These "holes" in the program are called *trap doors.*

Many times these are overlooked in the final product, leaving a computer criminal an easy path into the program, again by-passing security controls. In other words, no matter how many locks are on the front door, if the back door is flimsy it can easily be kicked open.

They probably won't admit this to the public, but major computer manufacturers also leave trap doors in the operating system for their underknowledged technical support people. Thus, if a criminal sort knows the operating system trap door, he/she has access to far more computers than those running a specific application.

Trojan Horse. Ancient Troy fell, so the poet Homer assures us, because the defenders were stupid and pulled a huge wooden horse full of Greek soldiers within their walls. Trojan horse programs use exactly the same concept. They're normal looking—often trusted, tried and true programs with *another* program concealed inside. The Trojan program will often appear to work correctly, but the concealed "bonus" program will be doing the programmer's bidding. This is the most common way computer-based frauds are perpetrated. It's also a way computer viruses are spread.

A Conspiracy of Silence

Readers of the computer industry trade press may wonder why magazines like *Time* and *Business Week* have recently devoted their cover stories to the security/virus issue when the trade publications make scant mention of the threat, if any at all. Normally, the computer press is at least a year—if not two years—ahead of general public awareness on computer-related topics.

Steve Jobs' new NeXT computer, formally announced in October 1988, immediately hit the cover of *Newsweek*. A new and exciting subject to the general public? Of course. But rumors and speculation surrounding Jobs' NeXT product had been bandied through the trade press for years.

There seems to be almost a stone (silicon?) wall in certain parts of the computer industry surrounding computer crime and security. IBM stoutly contends that the CHRISTMA.EXE program was *not* a virus (this depends, of course, on the definition of a virus as we shall see later). Certain industry gurus deny the existence of viruses in the face of overwhelming evidence to the contrary. One industry weekly suggested smirkingly that an MIS manager's best tool in the antivirus arsenal is a snappy memo, addressed to management, poised on the word processor for use after *Time, Fortune,* or the *Wall Street Journal* publishes another scare article.

And scare articles some of them may be. Most security or virus experts have at least one tale to tell of being interviewed at length by a reporter for a prestigious publication and having their words misunderstood or misquoted. Deadlines don't wait for technical fact-checking, especially when a reporter has a "hot" issue in hand. The more sensational it sounds, the better the publication sells. Security experts generally agree that the "information" promulgated by the popular press is, most often, inaccurate. But try to explain that in a four-column inch letter to the editor or, worse yet, in understandable terms to the CEO who just read the story.

Why is the trade press avoiding, ignoring and/or playing down the issue? We don't know, but we can make some educated guesses. The success of any publication is directly tied to its advertising revenues. These can be respectable. In many industries, including the world of computers, massive amounts of print and accompanying advertising are distributed "free" to hundreds of thousands of "qualified professionals." The qualification? The demonstrated ability to purchase the advertisers' products.

Clearly, if the purchasing public becomes fearful or afraid of a class of products, sales revenues will drop. If sales revenues drop, the advertising budget will be reduced. If the publication asking for those precious advertising dollars contributes to the drop in sales through confirming the public's fear in open print, the dollars will probably disappear faster than Dorothy did from Kansas. That's one possibility.

Another thought: Many a person has made a name for him or herself in the trade press by being early out of the gate and then parlaying connections and supposed inside information coupled with some level of technical expertise into the print inches of a featured column. The resulting credibility is sometimes then parlayed into green dollars from sales of the columnist's proprietary products or speaking engagements. Editors and reporters are journalists. The guru columnists are supposed to have "the Right Stuff." What if they don't? Will they tell? Whom can the experts ask without losing face?

One well-known columnist has, so far, flip-flopped at least three times on the virus issue, saying in essence, first, "Eek! Viruses! Run for cover!" This was followed later by, "Viruses are a media hype." And now, "Viruses are a clear and present danger."

If the expert columnists don't know, how can an editorial direction even begin to be established? If a computer publication's editorial staff suggests, clearly stating, "Fear what might happen to your computer and/or data," it's a good bet that the business side of the publishing house would strongly recommend concentrating on an in-depth review of floppy disks available in eight colors or more costing less than 25 cents each.

So, while a hot subject on the UPI and AP wires these days is that of computer viruses, you don't see a lot about it in the trade press. Such prestigious national magazines as *Time* and *Business Week* have devoted covers to viruses and run lengthy feature articles, but go to your local newsstand and look through the computer magazines. Few ever mention viruses, and certainly through the date this chapter is being written, *none* have given the subject the sort of emphasis the popular press has.

Simple human nature is the answer. If your company is in the business of selling computer hardware or software, you certainly don't want the public to become *afraid* of your product. Since you are paying computer magazines big advertising bucks, your concerns tend to become their concerns.

Prevention of Computer Crime

We'll go into computer crime prevention in more detail as this book progresses. To give you a summary, however, specialized detection techniques can be implemented for programs that might be subject to tampering. There are also a wide range of tests that can find logic bombs and determine if a program is a

Trojan horse. None of these, however, are totally foolproof.

The best security is simply to limit access as much as possible. A computer system is like your home while you're away on vacation. You can't keep a really determined burglar out, but you can use locks and alarms to make his access so hard that entry is delayed as long as possible. The thief will either give up because it's taking too long to get in, or still be pounding away at the lock when the cops arrive.

The coauthor of this book, during his Military Police days, was responsible for physical security on a number of sensitive facilities, including those where large quantities of weapons were stored. The technique the Army used was called "triple barrier" protection. This means simply that there are three "locked doors" before an intruder can gain access to anything valuable.

Conclusion

So far we've just touched the surface to the many ways a computer crime can reach out and grab you. The following chapters are not so much to show you more ways, but to help you master the interdependencies of computer security and protect yourself. We look at physical, data, and communications security on computers and how all of these melt together for an overall security protocol.

Your employees, fellow workers, or that smart kid down the block will always invent new ways to implement computer ripoffs. There's no way you can keep up with their sheer criminal creativity, so don't worry about it. Institute proper levels of security and slow them down enough so tampering can be prevented or, in worse case, detected in the early stages before much damage is done.

3
TECHNICAL LIMITATIONS

In the parlance of the prize-fighting ring, computers overall and *especially* personal computers—be they IBM or Macintosh—have a "glass jaw." PCs "lead with the chin" due to the delicacy of their file structure. This chapter explains these technical limitations in simple language, discusses how these weaknesses affect security, and shows how to work around them in your overall security plan. Security, after all, depends in great part on how you *use* your equipment.

Chuck Gilmore, of Gilmore Systems in Los Angeles, tells an amusing story. Chuck recently saw a gentleman park a Rolls Royce on Rodeo Drive in Beverly Hills and embark on a shopping excursion. This substantial-looking gentleman was accompanied by a Doberman carrying a wallet in his mouth. Obviously, we have a good use of security equipment here, as any survivor who has ever attempted to take a wallet (or anything else) from a Doberman can attest.

Most of us, it's true, couldn't care less about all the technicalities in this chapter. However, it's to our benefit to have at least a basic familiarity. A little knowledge could easily save hours of work and thousands of dollars in damage. Yes, it *really* can, but no computer manufacturer or salesperson is going to scare away a possible sale by saying so. Since you've already purchased this book, we know you're interested in security. Knowledge, as we've said before, is *power*.

This chapter concentrates on the IBM and compatible machines since (despite Apple's continuing valiant efforts for the Macintosh) IBM dominates the business environment. Later on, we'll have specific Macintosh security information.

Our thanks for most of the material below goes to Andy Hopkins, Vice President for System Development of Panda Systems.

PC Weaknesses

The memory of the system itself is the most vulnerable area of the personal computer to data destruction. Data stored in Random Access Memory (RAM) is subject to total destruction by a power failure, another program grabbing the memory locations already in use by a previous program, or a restart of the system (cold or warm boot) by the operator that clears memory.

The memory in most personal computers is a set of integrated circuit chips called dynamic RAM or DRAM for short. These chips are nothing more than thousands of small versions of the electronic devices, called *capacitors,* connected to transistors. A capacitor consists of two conducting surfaces separated by a small nonconducting area. As electrons flow to one surface, others are repelled from the other surface. This causes one surface or side of the capacitor to be charged. But the charge on a capacitor will, over time, leak or bleed off unless it's recharged.

To keep the charge from bleeding off the memory capacitors, a computer must refresh the charge at periodic intervals. In the IBM-PC the memory is refreshed every 15 microseconds. If the power is disconnected for just a fraction of a second, the capacitors will loose their charge and the data stored in memory is *forever* lost.

A little technical extra: When power "browns" but does not fail (the voltage drops due to overload), strange things can happen in RAM as memory begins to clear but does not finish the job. The system will begin to behave in bizarre ways and a user just might scream, "VIRUS!!!" A good clue to RAM scrambling caused by a power "brown" is a weird system date or time.

Floppy Disks and Hard Disks

Almost all personal computers used in business or for pleasure have some form of mass storage device for programs and data. Typically, a personal computer in a commercial situation has one or two floppy disk drives and usually a hard disk. Next to RAM, the mass storage device, be it a floppy disk or hard disk, is the second most vulnerable area in today's personal computer. Perhaps it is our reliance on the permanence of the data stored on the hard drive or disk that makes these devices the most critical peripherals in the entire system. Data lost here is often gone forever. Yet the data stored on a typical disk or hard drive is always susceptible to operator error, hardware failure, environmental conditions, power failure at a critical moment, and deliberate destruction by sabotage.

The typical user is blissfully unaware of the underlying structure used for mass storage of data on a disk. The IBM-PC, introduced in 1981, set a standard used by the majority of personal computers whether they wear the IBM label or not. The Disk Operating System, usually called simply DOS, was designed to make the user independent of the technicalities involved in saving and retrieving data from a disk. When we look at a monitor, all disk devices look the same whether they be a 5¼-inch disk, a 3½-inch disk, or a multimegabyte hard disk. What the user sees is the tip of a multilayered iceberg of programs, each more specific to the hardware than the next.

The user may learn that a program called 123.EXE exists on the disk by typing a DIR or directory command on the keyboard. He or she only needs to know that entering 123 will start that program and run it until a certain set of commands ends the program and returns the user to the familiar A:> or C:> prompt on the screen.

The screen prompts—such as A:> or C:>—that we're accustomed to come from a program called COMMAND.COM. This program is automatically started whenever the computer is turned on with either a system disk in the A: drive or with a hard drive configured for DOS. While COMMAND.COM is all that's visible during operation, it's not the only program in memory. COMMAND.COM passes information to IBMDOS.COM which passes information to IBMIO.COM, which then passes information to BIOS, which then passes information to the disk or hard drive. The information is finally passed back up the chain to the user who can remain completely unaware of and unconcerned with the process.

27

How Disks Work

Let's look at the process from the other end, starting with the floppy disk. Since the hard disk can be thought of as nothing more than an extremely large disk, let's take a disk apart and see what makes it work. (Don't worry, they're cheap.)

Inside the square cover of the disk is a thin platter of plastic film covered with a magnetic oxide. This is the same material used to make audio tape in the standard cassette recorder. Almost all disks are covered by the magnetic oxide on both sides even if it is labeled as a single-sided disk. It's easier to manufacture with the oxide on both sides, but single-sided disks are only tested on one side. This thin wafer of oxide-coated plastic sits in a square Teflon®-coated sleeve. The circular opening in the center is the drive motor hole.

When the door of the disk drive is closed or the handle is engaged, two things happen. One, the drive shaft is firmly engaged in the center of the disk wafer, and two, the read/write heads are moved against the magnetic oxide along the large slot in the front of the cover. (Or rear depending on your point of view.) There are two other irregularities in the outer covering of the sleeve. The small hole is known as the *index hole* and if the inside wafer is turned by hand, you can see a small hole in the inside that lines up once each revolution with the outer hole. The other irregularity is the notch in the lower left (or upper right) of the sleeve. This is the write-protect notch. Mechanical linkage inside the disk drive prevents the record mechanism from activating if this notch is closed.

The smaller disks used with the PS/2 line work on much the same principle as the larger 5¼-inch disk. However, the sleeve is made of hard plastic and the magnetic material is covered by a metal "door" which opens when the disk is inserted into the drive. The large Winchester-type hard drives used on most systems have several platters of magnetic disks stacked on top of one another, with several read/record heads on either side. A hard disk will not have the write-protect notch. A hard drive can *always* be written to (unless a special program like WPHD.COM is implemented—WPHD standing for Write-Protect Hard Disk). This type of program provides a software equivalent of a write-protect notch.

When produced by the manufacturer, the magnetic material on the disk has no orientation at all. There is no information whatsoever on the disk. It cannot record any useful information until certain steps are taken to magnetically divide the disk into small compartments known as sectors. Most users are familiar with the FORMAT command. Here's what happens. In order to find information on the disk quickly, it is magnetically compartmentalized into areas called sides, tracks, and sectors. The FORMAT command takes care of the nasty details of marking each compartment's name so subsequent reads and writes can find the right place on the disk.

Each side of the disk is divided into 40 round tracks. Each track is further divided into eight or nine sectors. The original PC disks had only one read/write head and each of the 40 tracks was divided into eight sectors. Each sector could hold 512 bytes of data. Thus the original disk could hold 512 bytes per sector times eight sectors per track times 40 tracks or 163,840 bytes. Later versions used nine sectors per track and both sides of the disk for a total of 368,640 bytes. A byte of data is eight bits—a convention set by IBM in the early days of computing. A bit is a binary digit that has only two states, on or off, like a light switch.

If you lined up eight light switches, you could flip each one only two ways, but there would still be 256 possible combinations ($2\times2\times2\times2\times2\times2\times2\times2 = 256$). When a disk is formatted, the track, side, and sector address information is recorded on the magnetic material so each sector can be accessed randomly without reading the entire disk sequentially. A small stepper motor moves the read/write head to the proper track position and then each sector's address appears under the head as the disk rotates in the sleeve. The index hole mentioned above can also be used to find the first sector on the track as it passes the head.

When a hard drive is formatted, the process is the same. However there may be two or more platters, each with two sides and many more than 40 tracks per side. A hard drive track is also typically divided into 17 sectors per track instead of only 9. Since the unit is sealed, and can spin faster than a disk, much more information can be recorded in the same space. Once the addressing data are recorded on the disk, it can be then used to store programs and data. The actual transfer is handled by software in the lowest level of the iceberg.

Read-Only Memory (ROM) in the PC family contains all the programs necessary to write to and read from the floppy disk or hard disk. All the ROM needs to know is which disk, which side, which track, which sector, whether to read or write to that sector, and at what memory address to get or store the data from that sector. This is where the next highest level of the operating system takes over. The program named IBMBIO.COM (or IO.SY on some MS-DOS computers) is the program concerned with Input/Output (I/O). It is this program that converts from physical addresses to logical addresses and vice versa.

To be able to locate the data on the floppy or hard disk, there has to be some form of cataloging or indexing. Therefore the logical organization of the disk is into files that occupy one or more clusters which, in turn, occupy one or more sectors. A typical file may be much larger than can be placed into one 512-byte sector; therefore some method must be used to designate which sectors contain the data from that particular file. Although there are many methods for doing this, here's how PC and MS-DOS do it.

File Structure

A portion of the disk is set aside for a listing of which files go where on the disk. This area is known as the *File Allocation Table* or FAT and it occupies predetermined specific sectors on each disk. The control of the FAT over disk data is such that if incorrect information is ever written to these sectors, all data will effectively be lost on the disk. Although the data are still there, they are as lost as Tom and Becky in the cave. The FAT is so essential that it's actually recorded twice on each disk. The disks are so reliable, that no program accesses the second copy of the FAT—not even DOS.

The original designers of DOS found that in order to allocate each sector on the disk, a minimum of two sectors would be needed for each file allocation table. A single-sided disk contained 320 sectors. Since each byte can only represent 256, two bytes would be needed to represent 320. Therefore two bytes times 320 sectors would take 640 bytes. Since each sector held only 512 bytes, it would take two sectors to represent the FAT. But this would cut down the amount of the user's data that could be held on each disk. So much for IBM's byte equals eight bits.

A byte and a half *could* contain a number up to 4095, more than enough needed and take only two thirds the space. Each sector of 512 bytes could contain 768 entries which would be more than enough. Therefore one sector was designated as the FAT and another as a backup (remember that word). When DOS expanded to double-sided disks and hard disks, there were too many sectors to allow each sector to have its own entry in the FAT. Thus the concept of clusters was invented so each entry in the FAT was a cluster of two, or in the case of the hard disk, 4 consecutive sectors. Subsequent DOS releases added the 9-sector-per-track disk and thus the FAT had to be expanded beyond the original single sector. On some hard disks up to 82 sectors are needed to hold the FAT.

IBMBIO neatly converts cluster numbers to side, track, and sector as needed by the ROM. Everything is in readiness for the user and the next logical step is to name each file according to some naming convention. A DIR or directory command shows not only the user-assigned names but other data about each file on the disk. DOS allocates several sectors of each disk as a directory which is, essentially, a catalog of the files on the disk.

Each entry consists of an eight-character (byte) filename and a three-character extension name which typically gives useful information about the type of file (PAYROLL.WKS, RESUME. DOC, XMASCARD.DBF). There is also one attribute byte that indicates whether the name is a volume label, a subdirectory, a regular file, or is hidden from directory searches. Ten bytes are unused and reserved for future use, four bytes are used to mark the date and time the file was last written to, four bytes are used to indicate the size of the file, and two bytes are used to indicate the starting FAT number.

Added up, each directory entry takes 32 bytes. Each disk sector can hold 512/32 or 16 entries. The original eight-sectored disk reserved four sectors for the directory. The nine-sector-per-track disk reserves seven sectors for the directory and many more sectors are reserved on the typical hard disk. After the FAT, the directory is probably the most crucial data area on the disk.

When a new file is created, DOS checks the directory to see if the filename already exists. If it does, the FAT entries for that file are cleared and marked as usable by another file. Contrast DOS' confidence in the user to most applications programs that announce the existence of a file with the same name and politely inquire whether you wish to overwrite it and whether you are *really* sure. The same procedure is used when a file is erased. The sectors used by the file are not immediately overwritten, but the FAT entries are marked as available for use. As clusters are needed by the newly created file, they're allocated from the pool of free entries and the FAT is updated to reflect the new file's usage of the disk. All the decisions as to where to put the new file are made by routines in DOS.

When a file is erased, the FAT entries are marked as usable and the first letter of the filename in the directory is replaced with a special character, usually a *sigma*, or Greek E. The crucial starting FAT number is left intact *as is the data contained in the file.* Most files erased with the DOS ERASE or DEL commands can be recovered with utility programs that recreate the original directory entry and FAT entries.

Sometimes something goes wrong. A file's directory entry can be deleted, but the FAT entries for that file may remain allocated. This is reported by the DOS program CHKDSK.COM as "*n* unallocated clusters found in ? chains." CHKDSK provides an option to clear these clusters as usable by other files. Another, although rarer, error is for two files to have the same cluster in their allocation chains. CHKDSK reports this as "cross linked files." Copying each file to another filename and then deleting the original files will clear up most cross linking. However, one file will contain a cluster that does not belong to it and will probably be unusable.

Sometimes a user goes wrong. We know the FAT is specific to the data on a particular disk. If a user picks up data from a floppy disk to use in an application running on another drive, does so and copies it back to the same disk in its new form, no problem. What if the user, for reasons unknown (that's why they call it an accident) *swaps floppies* before closing the data file? The FAT of the first disk is written to the second one. Whoops! A survey done by Panda Systems at one small installation of a Fortune 500 company showed data loss due to floppy swap occurring at least once each day among less than 500 users. This led to the creation of a utility called *WriteGuard™* which prevents damage due to a mistaken disk exchange.

Besides the Directory and the FAT, there is one other reserved sector on each disk—the boot sector. This is typically the first sector on the disk and it contains information about the disk and a short program that begins to load IBMBIO.COM when the computer is first started. Like all other sectors on the disk, the boot record can be written to and changed. Although the short program that the FORMAT command places in the boot record loads the operating system from the disk, it can easily be made to load another operating system as some game programs do, or any other program, such as a virus or a Trojan horse, which could take control when the short boot program is finished.

From a security point of view, the 512 bytes contained in the boot record may be the most crucial to the operation of the computer system and the most vulnerable to attack. Taken together, the boot record, the FAT, and the directory occupy seven or more sectors on the disk. *All* of these sectors are recorded as entries in the boot record. DOS uses this information to translate from FAT entry to side, track, and sector information.

System Programs

The next tier in the DOS structure is the program called IBMDOS.COM. This program is loaded at startup after IBMBIO.COM and contains routines to work with files and other tasks DOS can perform. These are the routines that read the directory and request Input/Output operations—an *I*nput from the disk or direct *O*utput to the disk through IBMBIO.COM. Most user applications access the many DOS services through this program.

The program most familiar to users and present on all DOS computers is COMMAND.COM. This is the program that interfaces directly with the user, accepts keyboard input, and displays the output on the screen. COMMAND.COM loads and runs other application programs and regains control of the computer upon completion of the application.

Taken as a whole, here's how all these programs work together after the computer is turned on. First, a routine in permanent memory (ROM) checks the computer's system to make sure all is functioning properly. This POST (Power On Self Test) includes the familiar *beep*. Next the drive named A: starts to spin and a search for the system files begins there. If a disk containing operating system files is in the slot, *and the door is closed*, the first sector of track one on side one is loaded into memory and control is passed to it.

If the disk in A: does not contain the system files, an error message "Non-System disk or disk error. Replace and strike any key when ready" appears. If a disk is not loaded because the operating system is on the hard drive, or the door is opened and a key is struck after the error message, the first sector of the hard disk is loaded. This initial short program looks at the first directory entry, whether on the floppy disk or the hard drive, for the name IBMBIO.COM. When the file is found, that program is loaded and control passes to it.

IBMBIO.COM loads IBMDOS.COM and searches for the filename CONFIG.SYS. If the configuration file is found, it is loaded and the commands in it are executed one at a time. Finally, COMMAND.COM is located and loaded and control is passed on. COMMAND.COM looks for the filename AUTO-EXEC.BAT and AUTOmatically EXECutes the commands found there such as setting paths, defining a prompt line, or re-assigning a serial printer to a communications port. Next, the prompt is displayed, and the user is in control. Notice all the files that are loaded and run before the user can take control of the computer. When OS/2 is being used, even more programs gain control first.

When COMMAND.COM or an application program (such as a word processing, a spreadsheet, or other application) is running, most file requests work their way up through the DOS hierarchy from the program to IBMDOS to IBMBIO to BIOS to disk and back down again. However, since the entry points to each of these routines are published, any program can be altered to bypass one or more of the upper levels. Sometimes this is done for speed since each level "up" becomes more and more general and the computations take more and more time. But it can also be done to destroy data on the disk.

A program that writes data to a *specific sector*, bypassing DOS, may overwrite data that DOS has already placed in that sector. Remember the random manner that DOS uses to assign new data to available spaces? Worse, a program can either intentionally or inadvertently overwrite the crucial FAT sectors making all data on the disk unfindable for all intents and purposes. The only recovery from this may be the tedious process of reformatting a disk and reloading the data from a recent backup.

Consider the nasty programmer who truly understands these inner workings of the PC. Remembering the order in which programs are accessed and loaded, and knowing the characteristics of certain files, an extra instruction or two is hidden in COMMAND.COM, CONFIG.SYS, or AUTO-EXEC.BAT. CONFIG.SYS would be a handy location, as it is a simple matter to *append* instructions to an existing file. The new instructions will be honored *last*.

"Install" programs for many software packages include a "write" to CONFIG.SYS to set the requirement for file and buffer availability needed by that package. Let's say your monster database program requires 20 files and 25 buffers available and your new software requires only 16 files and 8 buffers. "Install" will write FILES=16 and BUFFERS=8 at the *end* of CONFIG.SYS. The lines in CONFIG.SYS will be read and loaded in order, top to bottom. Your new software will run just fine, but your data base will stop dead in its tracks and return some disquieting messages. You may again be tempted to scream, "EEK! A VIRUS!"

A little nip from an install program requires only thinking about it for a minute and a quick edit of CONFIG.SYS to get things back to normal. A recovery from a big bite (byte?) from a computer criminal could take far longer.

Conclusion

Time to be frank and/or earnest.

Computer data storage is a lot more vulnerable than most people realize *or are told*. The problem of computer security, viruses, bombs, and Trojan horses aside, there are still numerous operator errors and equipment malfunctions that can scramble the contents of a floppy disk or even an entire hard disk in less than a second. That's why most thoughtful managers and consultants—as well as the developers of "shell" programs that are supposed to make using the operating system easier—tweak things just slightly to disenable the command that would allow an unthinking user-format of a hard drive.

Salespeople, columnists, consultants, and others connected with the computer industry tend to not mention or, at best, gloss over this vulnerability. It has been the experience of the writers—wearing their computer consultant hats—that most people are simply unaware of how precarious their data storage really is and have, themselves, learned it the hard way.

The computer industry has greatly downplayed the areas in which computers can be unreliable. Backup and DOS-level maintenance are not stressed or often taught. Confused and frustrated end users waste hours upon hours attempting to recover (or trying to) because of the "conspiracy of silence" that we discussed in Chapter 2. Every file read/write operation is an accident waiting to happen.

We'll cover DOS-level maintenance and backup procedures and methods later, to the extent that they relate to overall security.

4
PHYSICAL
SECURITY

If potential criminals can't get to your computer, they can't
steal it, and they sure can't mess around with the data it contains. This chapter is about methods for securing the physical
integrity of computer systems in the home, in the small office,
and in the larger-system arena. Locks, keeping the computers in
a safe place, and limiting access are three important parts of
computer physical security.

Let's look at some of the components and/or methods to
secure hardware and data. The way you or your company
work, physical layout, and budget will determine which meth-
od(s) provide the most "bang for the buck."

Physical Hardware Security

As kids we learned about such important security devices as bi-
cycle locks and locks on our diaries. Through our own experiences, or those of our friends or acquaintances, we found that
not chaining our bikes to the rack could result in no bike. Not
locking the diary resulted in a rotten little brother—who
couldn't ride around on his stolen bike—disclosing our secrets
to those from whom we would most wish to keep them. In this
respect, nothing has changed over all the centuries that Mankind has roamed this planet. Remember our cavewoman and
her shiny pebbles? Leave something unguarded and someone
will quickly appropriate it for fun, profit, or our own discomfort.

Our computer hardware, like all our other possessions, especially those of great value that are relatively portable, falls
into this category. However, the problem is actually of greater
scope than with most things we own. If someone swipes our
bike, we can eventually get another one and, in the meantime,

simply grit our teeth and accept the fact that it temporarily takes longer to get from point A to point B on foot. But a computer thief may be taking something intangible as well—megabytes of our sensitive and important *information.* This is a theme we keep singing loudly in this book—*information is valuable.* Hence, physical security of equipment, since that hardware stores or is used to retrieve our information, is of far more importance than just "chaining up our bikes."

The suggestions below cover ways you can implement physical security for computer equipment. Again, it will be obvious to you that some of these are appropriate only for an office environment, yet many of them apply to your personal machine at home as well.

Controlled and/or Guarded Access to Work Areas

Leaving computers out where anyone can access them is asking for trouble, whether unintentional or malicious. Some youngster, trying to bring up *Pac Man* while you've gone to the rest room, could wipe out an important spreadsheet.

In fact, a young person would be more likely to close out your spreadsheet file properly than the clutzy co-worker from down the hall. (The kid would score higher on *Pac Man,* too. People under 20 have grown up with computers, and they are generally more apt to use them correctly than a cybernetically-illiterate adult. But not always).

One programming consultant enjoys telling this "detective story:"

His company had developed an elaborate database program for a public agency. The agency's budget was limited, but he was just starting out and was happy for the work and experience. The agency's function: to keep track of all the state's drunk driving convictions and administer the rehabilitation programs required before an offender could get his or her driver's license back.

The agency's computer operator was a nice lady given to sensible shoes. Her continuing fear of the "magic box" had caused more than a few unnecessary support calls. This particular day, she called in a tizzy.

"There's no data!"

With a heavy sigh and heavier heart, the consultant proceeded to the agency's offices to show the dear lady *one more time* how to work the system. His heart grew even heavier when he realized the lady was right—there *was no data*. The file (OFFENDER.DBF) was still in place but was EMPTY. Excellent design procedures had included an almost automatic backup so the data could be restored—but *where had it gone?* The rest of the hard drive looked fine. Anyway, the agency was back in business.

The next morning, the dear lady called again, even more upset than the day before.

"There's no data!"

At the client site, it was discovered that this time even the *file* was gone! After restoring from the previous day's backup, Glenn returned to his office to put on his deerstalker hat. In 1984, the question of a progressive virus would have entered no one's mind as a probable cause, so the job was easier.

Clearly, the sweet lady was technically incapable of making these things happen. The entire office staff wandered through our budding Sherlock's mind—most of them wearing bifocals and cardigans. One face stood out. The young janitor, a high school student at a local school, had often talked to the programmer when they were both in the office late in the day. The youngster seemed to have not only a keen interest in things computerish but had talked at length about the computer course he was taking. Hmm.

It didn't take long to discover that one of the young janitor's friends had recently been arrested for underage drinking and driving, an offense that would have caused the offender to lose his drivers license until the age of 21. Confronted, the youngster admitted his misdeed. The agency did not prosecute but did terminate his employment. The consultant then instituted stringent security procedures for both the computer and its data, a rarity in 1984. Was our young friend acting in the spirit of friendship—or was he on the leading edge of computer crime?

So, especially in an office or other work environment *accessible* to the public, computers should be disabled (keyboard or other controls locked) when unattended. No one should be able to just walk into the computer area and "play." Office managers for smaller operations and security guards in larger businesses must be made aware that computers are the same as vaults containing gold—and in many cases, are actually more valuable and *easier to break into.* It is essential that all employees be aware of who *should* or *should not* be messing around with computers. And no employee should be afraid to ask someone questionable *just what it is* he or she is doing with a computer.

Combination Lock on Office Door

One method allowing easy access to a computer room for authorized personnel is a simple keypad-type combination lock on the door. This eliminates the need for issuing keys, keeping track of them, and dealing with "lost" keys. The manager also has the option of changing the combination at varying intervals (it does not pay to be regular in this type of precaution—randomness is more effective).

As with passwords, combinations can be very predictable and/or completely unguarded. When one of the authors worked at a small site of a large chemical company, new offices were opened, including a state-of-the-art computer room which featured a separate air conditioning and filtering system, special antistatic carpet with little copper tendrils woven in and every other device then known and available, regardless of cost. The company clearly believed in the majesty of data processing.

Returning from a European business trip late one night— the new computer room had been completed during her absence—the author decided to pick up the portable computer stored in this Taj Mahal. She intended to take it home and make the required trip notes and reports since jet lag would not allow sleep for another six to eight hours.

Gaining access to the professional office plaza required a special card, sign in, and visual recognition by the guard. Entering the building required another card and three separate keys. Getting into the new computer room with its state-of-the-art access control? Only the recollection that the MIS manager was three years older than she. 19xx was the combination.

Such tricks as issuing a new combination only to certain

employees can tell you whether they're guarding it properly. If a person who is supposed to be able to gain entry comes to you for the new combination, fine—but if you see others in the computer area working, this means that one of the recipients of the new combination leaked. Or maybe they just walked in with someone else.

This may all sound like a bit of paranoia—or even underhanded—to many, but it becomes necessary at times to emphasize just how overwhelmingly important computer security is. Most importantly, even if they think you an officious prig, it certainly prevents them from taking security precautions lightly. Besides, a good manager should have the skills to make such necessities understood and accepted—unless he or she really is an officious prig, of course (a security problem in itself).

Identification Markings on Hardware

If your hardware can be identified as *yours*, the chance for recovery in case of theft goes up. That's why parents write their children's names with magic marker on the socks that go to camp; and none of us has ever spent $50 on a new baseball glove without marking it as ours. The more visible and harder to eradicate, the better. If markings are obvious and *ugly*, no sane thief is going to want it, the difficulties in fencing would be too great. Another discreet ID in a hidden location is also a good idea, in case someone does figure a method to erase the outer markings.

Alarm Systems

A good alarm exists not so much to call attention to a break in as to prevent one in progress from continuing. Its true purpose is to scare the thief and send him running. Something as simple as a siren that *blasts* if the system unit is moved or as complex as infrared or ultrasonic motion detectors can be used. Airline or retail store type walk-through detectors are useful for large installations.

Cabling

Cabling hardware components to each other and to a solid object is also a good idea. Aircraft cable, which is galvanized and hard to cut but still flexible and easy to work with, is an excellent choice. In fact, cabling techniques are exactly the same principle we used when we were young and chained our bikes to the rack at school. Cabled equipment is not thief proof, but locks and cables *slow* greedy miscreants down! Here we have the *real* secret of all security—be it protecting your computer, your bank, your herd of cattle, whatever. The secret is this:

It is impossible to absolutely prevent something from being stolen if the thief *really* wants it, but you *can* slow down the process so much, and make the task so difficult, that any intelligent thief will leave in disgust in search of easier pickings. This is what you want to keep in mind when designing a cabling system. And lock up the bolt-cutters you use to trim the cable with, huh?

There are several companies that can supply everything needed to firmly tie down personal computer systems. One of these is Secure-It Inc. (18 Maple Court, E. Longmeadow, MA 01028, 1-800-451-7592). For $54.95 (postpaid) you get a heavy duty ten-foot steel cable and the necessary hardware to secure up to six units. The fasteners supplied attach to equipment without drilling, using existing screws. The cable passes through fasteners, preventing its removal. the cable is then locked, and locks for multiorders may be keyed the same or differently. The manufacturer claims that over 80 colleges now use their product.

Another way of securing units is the PadoLock™ security system from Doss Industries (1224 Mariposa, San Francisco, CA 94107, 1-415-861-2223). Instead of cables, this lock-down system consists of two interlocking 16-gauge steel pads. One pad secures to your workspace, the other to the bottom of your equipment. The two pads uniquely interlock with four steel rods, one on each side. Two "satellite" pads allow you to customize the security system to the size of your equipment.

Padolock, says the manufacturer's literature, "secures without drilling, and without expensive installation charges."

It uses the latest in high bond acrylic adhesive technology

and is claimed to secure equipment against over 10,000 pounds of force in an attempted removal. Provision is also provided for bolting the pads to your work table, thus providing double protection. This type of system gives the same protection as cabling without being quite so unsightly. The price is $89.95 with quantity discounts offered.

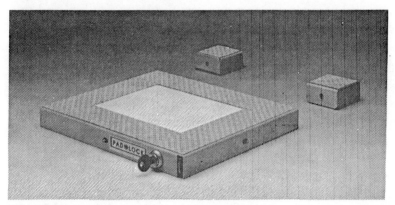

The PadoLock system consists of two interlocking 16-gauge steel pads. One pad secures to your worktable, the other to the bottom of your equipment. A lock allows the equipment to be removed for service. (Photograph courtesy Doss Industries.)

A Macintosh secured with PadoLock. This provides a neater appearance than cabling. (Photograph courtesy Doss Industries.)

Doss Industries also makes a unit called Control Power that puts a keyed switch in the power cord to any piece of equipment. Without the key, says the manufacturer, your equipment cannot be turned on and nobody else can access your data. Control Power is designed to work with any device that has a removable power cord.

There are numerous other manufacturers who also supply cabling and other lock-down devices. Find one you like and secure that valuable equipment.

Vaults

The top of the line in data storage is the concept of temperature and humidity controlled vaults which are now found in most major cities. It's a limited service, with no more than 50 such installations around the country. Sidney Craven, owner of The Vault, Ltd. in Wilmington, Delaware, entered the market in an interesting way.

His company was founded in 1982 to provide secure storage for such things as Mrs. Gotrocks' tiara and Admiral Moneybags' (U.S.N., Retired) extensive collection of rare stamps and coins. Dedicated to service, Mr. Craven offered something banks did not—a facility that's open 24 hours a day. To the working middle class among us, it may be hard to imagine a wealthy dowager dropping in at 3:00 a.m. to pick up a selection of jewelry or an elderly wealthy possibly requiring a quick look at his priceless collection before Sunday morning coffee. Within six months, though his service was very well accepted within the initial target market, Mr. Craven determined that he needed to expand his business in order that he might become as rich as his clients.

Calling proprietors of similar services around the country, it became clear that the real money was in providing data storage for computer installations. A pickup and delivery service was all that was needed to move into the high-tech world.

Today, The Vault provides secure data storage to a large banking community (many New York banks have moved their credit card operations to no-interest-ceiling Delaware), to the Fortune 500 companies that give Delaware the name of "corporate capital of the country," and to smaller companies. The majority of storage (about 60 percent) are tapes and disks of the banks' and corporations' mainframe and minicomputer generated data in active rotation. Smaller businesses' current backups account for most of the rest, with only about 5 percent of the media storage accounted for by escrowed source code.

Craven states that 90 percent of The Vault's clients can have backups delivered to their corporate doors in less than one hour, and he receives 40 to 50 such emergency calls each month. The reason for such emergencies is usually human error. As this book went to press, he was unaware of any clients who have lost data due to viruses.

The Vault has also considered the concept of *tele-vaulting* where the data would be transmitted to storage via telephone lines. Mr. Craven estimates the cost of secure telephone lines, the computers to receive the data, and the additional staff required for such a service would cost three to five times more than pick up and delivery by The Vault's uniformed employees.

Diana Rubin of DataVault Corporation near Boston confirms Sidney Craven's experience. Their clients break out approximately the same way in ratios of big businesses to small, number of emergency calls and, so far, no known "hits" from viruses. But just how did DataVault come to be an American success story? The proprietor, originally a security consultant, advised clients to make two copies of their microfilm records and store one in a safe place. (How long ago were records stored on microfilm?) The clients, trying hard to follow the expensive advice they had received, could find no suitable location for microfilm storage. And an industry was born.

Such costly storage is probably only indicated for giant entities or when the data involved is more precious than pearls. The everyday individual user is most likely not a candidate for these services. But managers of highly sensitive data, programmers, the owners of essential work product (authors, for example), or genealogy experts may rest easier knowing their work is safe, at whatever the price.

Locking Up Equipment

Placing spare hardware or software components under lock and
key is another of those obvious precautions. If equipment is
used infrequently, is light enough to be carried, and is not cabled
or chained to anything, and if outsiders have access to the area,
lock up that equipment. A good solid steel cabinet with roomy
shelves is excellent for this. However, if your cabinet is one of
the sheet metal variety found in most offices, you'll need to
padlock a chain around it for additional security. Otherwise, 30
seconds with a small screwdriver will pop it open, and your
new 60 megabyte tape backup unit, or 2400 baud external modem will waltz out of the building under someone else's arm.

Physical Data Security

This section anticipates and treads on the toes of the next
chapter, Data Security, just a bit. While there is a difference in
emphasis between the two, this clearly indicates the symbiotic
nature of security issues. In the next chapter we discuss protecting data mostly via software (executable program) means. Here,
we are more concerned with doing it by physical methods.
There is, however, also one exceptionally important common
denominator. Frequent backups.

An essential part of the physical data security equation is
disk operating system (usually referred to as DOS) maintenance. Protecting data means safeguarding it from far more
that just thieves—we must also protect it from the somewhat
sloppy way we often use our computers. Burglaries may occur
rarely, but there is a constant, everyday danger to the very existence of our hard-won data. More specifically, this includes corruption of chains and clusters as data areas on a disk are used,
reused, and used again.

On IBM and other MS-DOS computers, how often are
disks examined with CHKDSK which finds, and can correct,
this thievery by use? Not nearly often enough, if ever. Lost
cluster chains and files corrupted for a variety of reasons crop
up constantly on the best of systems.

If DOS-level maintenance is not done on a regular basis—
such as running CHKDSK with the /F option so lost chains
will be saved to files—any IBM or compatible file system is

eventually going to tear itself apart. This is a fact of life. Not just on IBM and compatibles, but on all computers. The disk is spinning (in the case of most PC hard disks) at perhaps 3600 rpm. The heads are whipping back and forth. There are millions of operations per second going on in the computer's memory. A momentary voltage surge, a minute mechanical slippage, an error in one of thousands of program instructions, and the data on the disk is ruined or damaged.

The point to be made and understood here is that computers are all too capable of fouling themselves up without any outside help. Because of this vulnerability, viruses and other security violations can quickly and easily do serious damage. In mere milliseconds!

Not doing proper DOS-level maintenance is a serious security violation in itself. If you lose large amounts of data because of not understanding and not performing basic maintenance and backup procedures, you are (pulling no punches here) *stealing from yourself!* Don't do it. Crime does not pay. Back up on a regular schedule and keep open chains and the like off your disks by running CHKDSK/F regularly. It's a relatively simple task to include such a command in AUTOEXEC.BAT for the seasoned user, or to institute a tech-check schedule for end-user workstations.

For the nontechnical person, you can add the CHKDSK command to your startup procedure by finding and editing the AUTOEXEC file with a word processor in ASCII mode. *Don't* use one like *WordPerfect,* for example, that puts in control codes (which will confuse the computer) unless you also understand how to convert the file back to ASCII format. With *WordPerfect,* Ctrl-F5 will do this for you. A word processor like *Sprint* will do all this automatically for you. Just call the file, insert a line containing only *CHKDSK,* and save the file. That's all there is to it. If, when you start up your system, CHKDSK discovers a problem, you'll want to investigate. If you're not technically oriented it's probably best to ask for assistance from someone who has worked with DOS-level maintenance. There are many good books on DOS, and it's a subject all PC users should become familiar with.

Here's an example of how important backup can be. A

friend of one of the authors has a very successful small publishing company. The excellent monthly publication he puts out is based on a single PC with a 30 megabyte hard disk. With the PC and its attached laser printer, he does all the typesetting for his paper and it comes out looking great—thanks to his many years of experience as an editor and today's technology. His hard disk contains all his carefully prepared programs to run his paper, all of his article inventory and, in short, everything that keeps his business going. Yet he had no backup. Worse, he had never run CHKDSK on the hard disk. Why? Because, like the majority of computer users, he believed he had no time to learn such "technicalities" and they might have been beyond him. "If it ain't busted, don't fix it!"

If someone breaks into the old house where he has his office (a five-minute job for someone with a nail file), and takes the computer, he would be out of business. The thief would not only steal the hardware, but his whole paper in one, easy-to-carry package. Should his hard disk fail, in essence the same thing happens.

To his credit, this experienced professional editor came to realize the importance of data protection in the form of backups. He now has *Fastback,* one of the better programs for quick disk-based backup, and has purchased the disks he needs to keep a copy of the files and programs on his all-important hard disk in a *safe* place. We'll make sure he has a workable backup protocol in place by the time this book comes out. After all, he's a friend and we'd hate to see him lose a few million bytes of words and programs simply out of inaction. And since we've used him as a *bad* example, we want to use him as a *good* example, too.

A friend of both authors, Ross Greenberg, with several fine programs (including *RamNet* and *Flu_Shot+*) to his credit, is always seen, even at the most formal and important meetings, carrying a backpack. A backpack may look a little strange with a $600 suit—but *back* is the operative syllable. Ross would *never* leave his livelihood unguarded in his midtown Manhattan apartment without a *back*up in his *back*pack.

Backing Up into Security

The first line of defense against physical loss of data—whether through theft, equipment malfunction, a major earthquake, or other unanticipated act of the almighty or lesser souls—is "good" backup. Having a "backup" merely means you have current duplicates of your important programs and files. This must be done on a regular basis.

There is an easy-to-understand method for a basic backup protocol. Use this method whether you're just copying a few files onto a floppy disk, backing up the hard disk (which can require a hundred or more disks), or using a tape backup system. It works for home or office machines and it's called the *rotating* method.

To begin, make *two* complete copies of the data to be backed up. One is to be kept near the operating position (but not too near), and the other is to be stored somewhere safe off site. For a personal computer in the home, the off-site location might be a strongbox or a wall safe, or at least some place where a casual search by an intruder would not find it and it would be protected from fire.

If the information in your personally-owned computer is as important to your livelihood as is that of the authors, you might want to have an additional off-site location somewhere out of the house or office—such as a safety deposit box at the local bank or even one of the climate-controlled vaults specifically designed for media storage and now available in larger cities and towns.

Next, determine a backup schedule. The frequency of the backups will probably be determined by how much work you're willing to *redo* and your compulsiveness/laziness factor. If, in the event of loss, you think you won't mind re-creating an entire week's work, weekly backups are okay. If you have to back up a large amount of data (a real hassle on floppies), you may want to take a chance and only do it every month.

When it's time to back up, take the copy that's near to hand and copy the current data over the old data. Then take it to the off-site location and exchange it for the "old" copy there, which now becomes the near-to-hand copy.

At the next backup time, this copy is made current and rotated to off site. Why do it this way? Well, what if you had only one copy—the one near to hand? "Something" happens to your system and the disk with your current data becomes lunch for a virus? You reach for the backup (conveniently near) and stick it in the machine, which *promptly* eats the backup as dessert! Want to guess what you have now? Right, nothing. Zip. Nada. A major boo boo hath occurred.

With the rotating approach, you really have a three-tiered system. There's the data in the computer, the copy near to hand, and the one off site to prevent it being casually reached for when the system malfunctions. Also, of course, the off-site data ensures that you don't lose anything—or much at least—if your home or business is burglarized and the computer stolen—along with the backup disks that were so neatly arrayed in that nice plastic box next to it.

Practical Backups

IBM recognizes the importance of backup, even though they and their many clone competitors don't stress it enough to new customers. A useful little item that comes along with the disk operating system on personal computers is BACKUP.COM. This program works well enough in its slow, tedious and clunky way. It allows the backup of a hard disk by prompting the user to insert disk after disk and automatically fills the floppy disks as well as it can from the selected files on another (source) disk. There is also the companion RESTORE program for those times when you have to load the programs and data back. No one with a 20 megabyte hard disk is going to be happy with this backup program for long. A tiny 11.2 megabyte external drive requires 24 disks and more than an hour's time for a complete backup!

Better are the commercial programs like *Fastback Plus* from Fifth Generation Systems (11200 Industriplex Blvd., Baton Rouge, LA 70809). *Fastback* features a data compression technology that reduces the number of floppy disks needed by as much as two to one. It is also considerably faster. *Fastback Plus* is a marvelous, well-crafted program. Your data-lost paranoid coauthor used it for some time as his only method of backup.

But if you have a very large system, even *Fastback* can take many disks and a long time.

If you have a 1.2 megabyte drive, *Fastback* may be somewhat more attractive, but still you're going to have those disks to swap. One of Panda's law firm clients uses *Fastback* to back up its accounting records *daily* onto no less than 26 1.2 megabyte floppies! Even though the time required is less than 15 minutes, it's a pain for the operator and, sadly, is frequently skipped in the rush at the end of the day.

You may find your backup schedule slipping too. Even if you just do an incremental backup (only those files that have changed) it's still a hassle and can be guiltlessly skipped if something else seems more important.

Tape Drives

Currently the *best* answer is to forget floppies for backup altogether and get a tape drive backup unit. Streaming tape is the quickest and most selective way to do frequent and accurate backups. When this technology was first released, one of the authors, through a Freudian slip—she was so impressed with the speed of the thing—recommended that one client purchase a "screaming" tape backup and, apprised of her error, corrected the proposal to reflect a "steaming" tape backup! (Some days, you just can't win.)

In an office, one tape unit can service several PCs and backups can be done by clerical-level employees during off-hours. PCs can even be programmed to back up automatically to the tape drive on, say, Tuesdays at 3 a.m. You can put the complete contents of two 20 megabyte hard disks on one 40 megabyte tape.

To a business, streaming tape backup is the way to go if the importance of backups is recognized and validated as part of the corporate initiative. But it also makes economic sense to the individual computer owner. These days, you can get a good tape backup unit (internal and external) in the $400 range and up from many of the mail order firms. Since *Fastback* and similar programs that are floppy disk based cost $100+, there's not that big a difference, especially when the savings in time and the ability to always have absolutely current backups is factored in.

A good streaming tape backup on a PC will do something like five megabytes a minute. On the coauthor's hundred megabyte system, a complete copy of all four hard disks takes just two tapes and less than 20 minutes. He now backs up the whole system every three days just because it's so easy.

And it's always a good idea to have a complete copy of your whole system. This way, should the unfortunate happen and everything gets wiped out, there is just one reloading job— as opposed to installing programs back in from their original disks (and trying to remember *how* they were set up in the first place), and then having to restore the data as well.

Large Systems

Managers of large installations should use all the criteria above in planning physical data protection protocols, plus those listed below that individuals might not necessarily need:

- Consider hard-coding a frequent backup requirement into applications that generate sensitive or essential data.
- Backups should encompass at least three generations of changes on a rotating basis. Always keep a separate backup of the system's program configuration (no data). This is also a help in setting up new PCs to your specifications.
- Keep an archive backup that's not in the regular tape or disk rotation. In case of a "hit" by destructive code, this backup may be essential in tracking down the culprit.
- Do not store backups near the workstation. A securely locked, fireproof storage place is recommended.
- Password-protect individual machines or sensitive applications. Remember that many password schemes can be by-passed by booting a PC from the A: drive. In our experience, there's a 50 percent chance of finding the password taped to the monitor or in the pencil drawer of the workstation.
- Telecommunicate data via modem to an off-site storage medium. Back up to an on-site "blind" machine (system unit only) via hardwiring.
- Install antistatic mats or carpeting.
- Use surge suppressors and evaluate UPS (Uninterrupted Power Supply) systems.

(Password protection and telecommunications security are covered in following chapters.)

Between the Devil and the Deep Blue Sea

Here's an actual case study that shows just how important physical security and proper backup protocols can be.

An executive with an international chemical company contracted for an elaborate personal computer system that would link his office in the Northeast with three plant sites on the Texas Gulf Coast, and the corporate sales office on the West Coast. The purpose was to transfer data about available products and sales.

The contracting company did its initial work well and carefully, mindful of the sensitivity of the data as well as the possibility of disaster if data were lost. Quite simply, the company would be out of one part of its business (at least temporarily) if the master system crashed and its competitive edge would be lost if the sales data were to fall into the wrong hands.

The hardware configuration included a streaming tape backup and an UPS system. Software included elaborate passwording schemes, multiple data integrity checks with each transmission over the phone lines, and safeguards against unauthorized use of the machines.

For the first year of operation, the data was also backed up by the executive's handwritten records. This duplicated everything on the system, just like he had done for years before.

Finally, after many months of system testing and tweaking, it was signed over to the client—a finished, working system, brought in under budget, and just what was ordered. A real computerization success story.

Well, almost.

One Thursday morning, the client unlocked his office door and, with horror, realized his computer was missing. And his modem. And his tape backup unit. Even the credenza where he stored his software and backup tapes was unlocked and open. Empty!

There is a moderately happy ending to this part of the story. The contracting computer company was working on speeding up the application and had copied the active database to use in testing only three days before. The source code and compiled code for the application had been properly escrowed and only two days of operation were lost—most of it lost while waiting for replacement hardware.

Once bitten and twice shy, the executive was fearful of another theft. He was chagrined at his apparent failure in the eyes of management to protect the company's capital assets. His comfort level with the operation of the software together with the efficiency of the contracting company in a potential disaster situation worked, sadly, to his detriment, and the physical security of the hardware became his top priority.

His options were limited. The great bulk of system data transmission took place overnight, so it was impossible to put the AT, the monitor, and the modem in a locked closet. But he could, and did, lock up the tape backup unit.

Out of sight, out of mind. His original protocol of daily tape backups faded away until the data stored on tape was several months old. A move to a new office brought disaster.

The perspicacious reader will immediately jump to an obvious conclusion—the AT was not properly set up for the move. Not so. The system was reinstalled at the new location without incident. It was, however, easy to leave the tape backup unit stored away as the new office was a little smaller and didn't provide quite the same amount of room for hardware. The application had run reliably for almost two years. False sense of security time, here.

Then the heat came on. Literally. The previously humid ambient air became bone dry. New carpeting became a breeding ground for static electricity. *Zap*! Data gone!

Once more, we have a happy interim ending. Most of the data still actually existed, although file structures in the computer had been scrambled. The File Allocation Table (covered in chapter 3) was no more. Three programmers worked 24-hour days over a holiday weekend to reconstruct what could be found. The $4,000 programming bill was submitted as charges for "Correction of Faulty End-User Interface," thus saving face for the beleaguered client.

This sad tale is a textbook case both for programmers and

consumers, and demonstrates not only the separate essential security concerns, but how external forces, such as carelessness and static electricity can ruin the best plans and protocols. PC security is symbiotic and requires the interlinking of many different concerns and practices.

But no tale should be without a truly happy ending. Sadder and wiser, the client and the consulting firm worked together to add new programming and procedures to both the hardware and software sides of the system.

Daily tape backups are now system-driven, tied to the application program's activity and the system clock. The executive, or his secretary, carries the tape home evenings and returns it in the morning. The first program data access activities after 00:01 and 12:01 end with a required write to the tape unit. A backup to disk is accomplished with the initial request to access the program on a new system "day" date. An RS-232 interface with a "blind" system unit (no monitor, no keyboard) is located in a locked closet. With each overnight transmission loop among the sites, a complete data backup is sent to a leased mainframe for storage.

"U" loops have been attached to the system unit, the printer, and the tape backup. They are chained to a loop bolted into the floor. The company's name and an identifying code have been engraved on all hardware in an obvious and unattractive manner.

Dangers to Data

Theft is not the prime danger to data loss. Carelessness, improper backup frequency, fire, water pipes freezing and breaking to shower your computer, a fire sprinkler system gone haywire and doing the same thing, and/or assorted Acts of God or the foul-ups by the computer uninitiated rank higher. Lightning storms are always good for some nice sharp voltage spikes on power lines which can crisp the innards of any computer. There are an incredible number of ways all your work can be lost in the blink of an eye, some of which have yet to be discovered—until the first data loss. So protect yourself with backups and the physical security procedures detailed at the first of this chapter. Now, we move on to look at using software to protect data.

55

5
DATA SECURITY

It may not seem so—while considering a $3,000 desktop PC or a $2,000 supertwist backlit laptop—but hardware security is, relatively speaking, almost incidental in overall computer security. The real gold in "them thar hills" is the data these machines contain. Whether it's your personal checking account or your employer's regional sales figures, you do not want some stranger to read, copy, or alter it. Serious trouble could result from data falling into the wrong hands. Loose lips not only sink ships, they can bankrupt individuals and companies, too. This chapter is concerned with *data* security.

Changing Times

In the 1960s and 1970s, data security in the business world was much easier to implement. Almost all contact with the computer occurred only through terminals hardwired into the system. These dumb terminals provided an easy method for MIS (Manager Information Systems) people to keep track of who was accessing what.

The computers themselves were sacred monsters that lived in special, highly guarded computer rooms. There was little contact by outsiders or even most company employees. Few computer-literate persons were around anyway. Large corporations did not concern themselves very much with data security.

Time, however, does not stand still. There is an old nautical term that is especially apt for what has happened in the 1980s—a *sea-change*. On the sea you may be sailing in a fog or a rain squall one moment and break through into sunshine the next. That's what happened in the 1980s—one moment we were in the restrictive age of big machines; then, suddenly, the personal computer caught on and we were in the glorious light of the Information Age. William Shakespeare unknowingly described this decade in his play, *The Tempest*, when he said:

> Nothing of him that doth fade
> But doth suffer a *sea-change*
> Into something rich and strange.

The "something rich and strange" is the incredibly widespread usage of the personal computer. Where in the past decade an MIS person with a large corporation might have had only perhaps 25 or 30 people in one department to worry about, he or she now has *thousands* of users, all with their semi-independent little PC fiefdoms, spread throughout the firm. What's more, the typical computer user today is no longer a data processing professional, but the whole spectrum of a company's employees from temporary office help right up to the Chief Executive Officer.

Some among both the top and bottom of this heap do not have the appreciation for computer data security that MIS people could want. In fact, many couldn't care less. The base of people who can now access any sizable company's information has literally mushroomed in just the last year or so. Opportunities for these computer users to make errors in data entry, or even to perform malicious damage and/or other unauthorized changes in data continue to multiply at an exponential rate. Incompetence and lack of training in computer usage are also causes of costly data and operational errors, and in system crashes.

The security problems that MIS managers of large corporations see are not necessarily in the same order as emphasized in the popular press. Robert T. Martinott and John M. Winton's article "Getting a Lock on Computer Security" in the October 28, 1987 issue of *Chemical Week* is an excellent overview of concerns within the chemical industry. The article reports that chemical MIS executives had identified five broad areas of concern: fraud, loss of confidentiality, inadvertent damage to data, malicious tampering, and physical damage to the hardware.

Ross C. Ahntholz, director of the Information Systems Department at Olin is quoted as saying: "We are more concerned

about the confidentiality of data than about financial loss
through computer fraud."

And a manager who preferred to remain unnamed said:
"Our biggest problem is not keeping our competitors from getting our cost data, it is keeping our marketing people from getting it."

Data Security is Complicated

Because of the wide proliferation of PCs in corporations now—
many of them tied into the corporate mainframe system—data
security is made incredibly more complicated by the fact that
levels must be established. The example above of keeping information from marketing people which might cause them to
"give away" profits is a good one. It all goes back to the well
established military principle of "need to know."

Personal data on employees, payroll information, customer
records, and more are also types of data that must be restricted
within a company. The real headaches for MIS executives
come from the structuring of access. Various people in the corporation need access to varying types of data in order to make
decisions, or otherwise properly perform their jobs.

If more people are allowed access, there is more chance
that a hotshot executive, whose 12-year-old son is three times
as computer literate as he or she, will inadvertently wipe out a
tremendous amount of important data simply because he or
she has no concept of how computers really work.

The smaller the company, the greater the "protection from
stupidity" problem. In a smaller company, an employee can
usually proportionally access a greater amount of the company's total wealth of information. In a "Mom and Pop" operation with just one computer, like a candy store, Pop can wipe
out the company's one hard disk in less than a second, destroying all accounting data for the last year.

As the article in *Chemical Week* says, "many chemical
MIS managers believe honest employees can find more ways to
damage computer systems and compromise sensitive data than
the cleverest criminals."

Let's look again at the five areas of concern expressed by

the MIS executives in the article mentioned above. They were: fraud, loss of confidentiality, inadvertent damage to data, malicious tampering, and physical damage to the hardware. All of these apply to any type of computerized operation where security is important, "Mom" is as much an MIS executive as is the vice president for Data Processing of a major bank.

From Mom up to the lofty vice president, the realization should be the same—*most* of the damage in these five categories is caused by *employees*, not by outsiders. Again, the popular press tends to really emphasize those relatively few (although certainly serious) crimes perpetrated by outside criminals and/or hackers. Yet, most computer crime or losses due to operator error is done by insiders. Pop, you see, has taken to playing the horses lately (rather badly) and always needs money. So he fudges the candy store's daily receipts and pockets the difference. If Mom doesn't have good computer security, it may take her a few days to catch on to this sweet little scam that Pop is perpetrating.

Larger companies with hundreds or thousands of employees have a correspondingly bigger problem. This problem isn't just in fraud, but in the other four areas as well. Leaking of confidential and proprietary information (whether intentional or not) is a common concern of large corporations.

Out of perhaps 20,000 employees, there are going to be a sizable number who simply do not understand data integrity and why it should not be divulged. Also, obviously, the more employees there are, the more chances exist for the last three problem areas—inadvertent damage to data, malicious tampering, and physical damage to the hardware.

One midlevel manager riding roughshod over sensitive lower-level workers could cause several of them to get even by destroying data. A temporary office worker who knows little about computers could mistakenly erase megabytes of data.

We discussed backing up data in the last chapter. It has been the experience of the authors, and this is borne out also in the *Chemical Week* article mentioned above, that one of the biggest problems a MIS manager faces is getting all these thousands of novice PC users to back up their data. While data processing professionals have a deeply ingrained compulsion to keep backups, the myriad of new users do not, nor do they understand the imperative reasons as to why this is absolutely necessary. They tend to be causal about it. And even when a backup is made, the disks are often left just lying around (an obvious security violation in and of itself).

"We give them procedures and policy statements, but until they have been burned a couple of times, they don't learn," said Richard V. Baker, director of information systems at Mobay Chemical.

Mainframe computer security is pretty well established by now. Such companies as IBM and the Cambridge Security Group have multilayered protocols that allow the MIS executive to precisely structure access. The awesome proliferation of personal computers into the workplace, tied together into networks, in many cases bypasses old corporate security protocols.

A company in today's Information Age—where thousands of PCs are scattered throughout the firm and act as workstations—has no *choice* but to institute the security protocols required by the Information Age's new and more widespread requirements. They have no choice but to train their people and try to make them see the overwhelming importance of computer security. Those companies who don't, stand to lose a lot of money and time.

While a good many MIS people would like to keep all sensitive data only on the mainframe system, this is not possible in today's world. The sheer convenience of semiautonomous workstations, like personal computers, will guarantee their continued proliferation. Computing in general is rapidly being taken out of the hands of data processing professionals and given to *everyone*.

Alas, unlike the old mainframe days when computers were accessed mostly by dumb terminals, today's personal computer workstation makes it easy for the user to copy proprietary data. Many workstations have printers attached, allowing printouts of data to be made, folded, and thrust into a perpetrator's pocket. The same applies in even greater measure to floppy disks. A file containing the equivalent of a good-sized novel (80,000 to 100,000 words) can be copied onto a disk in seconds and hidden as easily as a sheet of paper.

So, computer data security, in the long run, is really more of a people problem than a technological problem for the MIS manager. This is as true for the top computer jock at Chase Manhattan Bank as it is for Mom at the corner candy store. However, there are various software and hardware approaches that help people to be more conscious of computer security. We'll look at some of the principles governing software protocols next.

Software Protection of Data

The term *software* refers to programs. The actual physical computers themselves are *hardware*. Software, the instructions that take a computer through a sequence of programmed actions, is an essential part of a computer system. Hardware is just so many expensive high-tech boat anchors unless you have a program that will do the job *you* want done.

MIS executives (from Mom on up) can install programs to overcome some of the multitude of faults engendered by the single greatest weakness of computers—the humans who run them. Because of the lackadaisical attitudes the majority of computer users (mostly through lack of knowledge) have about computer security, they must be "forced" to employ good security protocols.

An "executive" computer program that refuses to let other programs be run unless security procedures are performed, is the best answer today. There is a wide variety of program types for this purpose—even some that single computer users can employ to protect themselves and their data.

Larger companies, with a programming staff (assuming the programmers are trustworthy and will not put "trap doors" or some sort of Trojan into the programs), can custom design their own data protection software. Smaller firms and individuals now have hundreds of choices in commercial, shareware, and public domain programs. In later chapters, we'll cover many of these specifically (with names and addresses as to where the programs can be ordered).

For now, let's look at some general concepts. Consider, for example, a utility that blanks the screen with a keystroke combination and/or after *n* seconds with no keyboard activity. You should be able to adjust the program so each user can describe an individual combination of keys to reactivate the screen. Remember: Such a program must be a TSR (Terminate and Stay Resident in RAM) utility and cannot conflict with other RAM usage.

Protect floppy-based data from unintentional destruction by adding a utility that prevents "floppy swap." If data is read from one floppy during an application and the disk is exchanged before the file is closed, at least one of the disks' FAT (File Allocation Table) will be destroyed, rendering the floppy disk unusable for all practical purposes.

If a system unit fails and must be serviced, evaluate the service provider. Sensitive data should *never* be entrusted to anyone outside your administrative structure. If budget must be considered, degauss the hard drive before sending the PC for repairs and use your backups to restore the data following repairs.

Protect data from killer code by installing disaster prevention utilities that check for changes that indicate its presence and prevent destruction. In addition, perform routine checks to ensure that only authorized and/or licensed programs are present on each machine. Install a utility that prevents copying (stealing) a licensed program.

Institute passwords and encryption of more sensitive information. There should be levels of access set up so a shipping clerk can access inventory information but not payroll. Executives must be allowed information they need for decision-making within their areas of responsibility but restricted from being able to run willy-nilly throughout the entire system. Levels can minimize losses through carelessness or purposeful criminal activity.

Passwords are the most common method of maintaining computer security, and one of the more easily abused. Not changing passwords at *irregular* intervals (as opposed to regular ones), carelessness of users in guarding their passwords, and the use of easy-to-remember (and, thus, easy-to-guess) descriptive passwords are just a few of the mistakes consistently made. We'll go into this more extensively in the chapter on encryption and passwords.

Software protection, on the downside, is not the ultimate. Because they are programs, most security software can be circumvented. True data protection can be achieved through the hardware, but this also locks the system into a rigid configuration that makes it difficult to use, and even more difficult to change. Software systems may occasionally be compromised, but at least it's much easier to institute a new (and, one hopes, better) protocol.

Security and Recovery

This is another way of looking at backups, and one that must be a part of overall data security protocols for everyone from single to corporate users. In the event that data is lost or altered, there has to be a way to recover it so business can resume.

Data processing professionals view this as being divided into three interrelated principles. The book *Computer Control* by Mair, Wood, and Davis (published by the Institute of Internal Auditors, Inc. in 1978) is one such source for these techniques. The principles are:

• Preventing losses.
• Detecting disasters or other losses early enough to minimize the loss.
• In the event of loss:
   Recovery of data
   Insurance that will cover the costs involved

These apply just as well to the single-computer user as to a 20,000-machine network. You prevent losses by having good backup procedures and following them *religiously*. You implement detection of disasters and attempts at unauthorized use of the system through software protection packages (more about specific packages later). You make sure data can be easily recovered by use of the three-tiered backup method described in Chapter 4.

Make sure your specific computer security implementations cover the general bases listed above. Chances are very good that an equipment malfunction, an operator error, or (though less likely) some sort of an attempt at unauthorized access will hit your system in the very near future. Unauthorized access, by the way, can include such things as computer viruses.

6
SECURITY OVERVIEW

Chuck Gilmore

Chuck Gilmore, owner of Gilmore Systems in Los Angeles, specializes in viral protection and all aspects of IBM's new OS/2 operating system, including security. Chuck's company publishes the FICHECK *and* XFICHECK *virus protection software packages.*

With the advent of computer viruses, Trojans, and disgruntled employees, there has been much concern lately over the topic of computer security—more specifically, *data integrity*. The data stored on your computer's disk system is your most valuable asset, whether you're an individual or megacorporation.

Mainframe Computers

The mainframe environment typically supports hundreds of terminals and people, ranging from casual users to programmers.

A large company I once worked for used to make daily backups of data on tapes. The tapes were duplicated and then sent to a remote site in another state for storage. This was part of the company's "disaster recovery" plan.

Each mainframe user possessed an ID and password to log onto the computer from any terminal. Since this particular company had over 400 terminals, only those terminals in the immediate vicinity of the physical computer accepted the proper IDs and passwords that allowed access to the mainframes at an operator level (operators could monitor jobs, cancel jobs, mount new disks, mount new tapes, and so forth). To gain entrance to the operator area, each employee had to insert a special keycard in the door lock. Once beyond the door, he or she was required to sign in, which was witnessed by the permanently stationed guard on duty.

Once signed in, the keycard opened the next door, which led to the operator area. As if this weren't enough, there was yet a third door that required another keycard (but not everyone with access to the operator area had access to the third door), which led to the tape library storage area and to the room where the actual computer was located.

I've worked in other places where employees could actually enter the company's computer room simply by knocking on the door. It was easy to befriend some of the naive workers who often weren't much older than high-school age, and in doing so, persuade them to allow access to the computer room. Their jobs consisted of mounting tapes, changing disks, and handling other sundry duties that required little to no knowledge of computers.

Mainframe security, as demonstrated, varies from company to company. Some companies are strict with security while others offer little to no protection for valuable data and equipment. The two companies mentioned here were, respectively, a public utility company that used strict security measures, and a main computing center for a major East Coast department store chain, that used very little security.

Predictably, computer operators for the two places were quite different. The department store suffered high employee turnover and most employees, even at the operator and system programmer level, were inexperienced and very young. Conversely, equivalent employees at the utility company were typically older and stable and had professional degrees, good salaries, and good benefits. As a result, the utility company had little to no turnover. And while eight was the shortest number of years of employment for any computer operator with the utility company, no employee had ever lasted that long with the department store facility.

This suggests that computer and data security are not employee problems, but rather management problems. Data corruption was unheard of in the well-managed utility company. Everyone at the systems, operator, and technical levels knew everyone else and any code written was reviewed by others.

As a utility company, records for nearly every electricity consumer in the state were held in the corporate computers, including dollar amounts for household consumption, but only a few employees had access to those records. Among the three mainframe computers, only one was available to the sensitive information held in a security authorized database. Access was obtained only by the use of special passwords and then had to be cleared through the operator. A programmer couldn't even attempt to get near the database without setting off warning messages on the operator's terminals.

Hiring young and thus often unstable employees, as did the ill-managed company, is like leaving keys in the ignition of a car parked in a high school parking lot—the thrill lies more in the *act* of stealing the car rather than in *having* the car.

In further support of the "young and unstable" employee theory, a recent *Time* magazine article portrayed typical virus writers as affluent young intellects (having affluence via their parents) in their late teens to early twenties who lack social skills and have no idea what it's like to struggle in the real world.

Microcomputers (PCs)

Referring back to the well-managed utility company, at the technical level on mainframes, only certain systems programmers had access to particular service calls (SVCs) and to certain "privileged" instructions. An SVC is the equivalent of an interrupt on a DOS-based personal computer; DOS-based personal computers have no equivalent in *real mode.*

Real mode is the term used to describe how the central processing unit (CPU) acts. In real mode, a program has access to anything and everything in the computer—there are no privileged instructions, no security doors, and no operators policing the activities. Because of this, a program can contain instructions to do *anything* it wants, which means a person, conceivably, can write a destructive virus or Trojan horse program in an evening, send it up to a bulletin board service (BBS) via modem, and in a very short time, affect the hundreds of people who will download the program onto their computers. Worse yet, if a downloader finds the program useful enough to take to work and thus gives copies to others at the company, the infection will spread even further.

The popular disk operating system (DOS) for IBM and compatible computers is a real-mode system. Any program can contain code to bypass it, and most programs do. For instance, "writing to the screen" usually means writing *directly* to the screen instead of through the operating system to gain speed.

Early PCs having 640K RAM and 360K floppy drives, and even ten-megabyte hard disks, were a real step forward. These days, the equivalent system can't be taken so seriously: Programs are becoming more complex and are demanding more disk space and memory with each wanting control of the entire computer.

TSRs

The ability to switch quickly between programs—not having to end one program in order to begin another—was made possible with the advent of *terminate and stay resident* (or *TSR*) programs. A TSR attaches itself to DOS and remains there taking up memory, waiting to come to life with the right sequence of keystrokes. Borland's *SideKick Plus* is an example of this type of program.

TSR programs take advantage of real mode by altering vectors to run their own instructions. Although some of these programs can be quite useful, they end up clobbering each other by taking up more and more memory and trying to control certain interrupts. Each wants to be installed last (changing the interrupts already altered by other TSRs).

Virus writers and others who gain satisfaction from data destruction take advantage of the TSR concept. Their programs typically change the interrupt in charge of disk I/O (input/output or reading and writing) and have the CPU run its own destructive code instead of the original intended code. Trojan writers take advantage of how easy it is to bypass an operating system by directly scrambling the *file allocation table* (FAT); then, the operating system can no longer decode the magnetic information on the disk. TSR *virus blockers* use the same concept: They change the interrupts to point to their own routines.

A virus program typically spreads itself onto other programs and since all programs are contained in files, those files
must be altered in such a way that the virus is able to clone itself. *XFICHECK,* with it's dual CRC/MCRC (Cyclical Redundancy Check), date, size, time, and attribute checks, looks on a
disk for changes. Of course, like any other detection system,
this one assumes you started with uncorrupted files.

XFICHECK can be used to detect changes—to programs
and other files—that shouldn't have occurred, and it can be
used as a complete file-tracking system for *suggesting* that
something such as a virus may have occurred within a system.
Companies and individuals can use *XFICHECK*'s complete
checks and reporting methods to determine what and when
something has changed—source code, data, programs, new directories, removed directories, hidden files, deleted or added
files, and even the boot record/partition table—*anything* that
has uncustomarily changed.

Now managers can check individual users' machines or file
servers to see any out of the ordinary or unauthorized changes:
Was John Doe really working on his coding project today, or
was he playing games? *XFICHECK* can tell how much change
occurred during John Doe's working hours by showing changes
in the game's data file—showing both the date and time of
change and the CRC/MCRC change—and by showing the size
of of his source code files after working on the coding project.
XFICHECK can be used on a daily, weekly, or monthly basis,
depending on a company's needs.

Hardware Security

If you're really serious about data integrity, hardware security is
probably the the best way of securing your entire data system.
Both the hard disk and system cover of the original IBM AT
could be locked with an actual key.

Another effective, although expensive, method is to allow
access to a system via keycards. A user inserts his or her
keycard into the keycard reader and the machine either permits
or denies access to it depending on the keycard. For security,
one company used a piece of hardware installed in the form of
a card. All commercial programs first checked for the presence

of that card and for the proper encoding on it in addition to a user-entered password. If the card wasn't found, the program simply went into an endless loop. The only way to end the loop was to reboot the system.

Information Integrity

If you're more interested in keeping valuable data from falling into the wrong hands (corporate secrets, proprietary code, and so forth), there are methods of protection that will involve some work on your part.

Data encryption has been used in many forms and flavors. Typically, you assign a key or secret password to an encryption or decryption program. The program scrambles the information in one or more files based on the key or password and then that key or password must be used to restore the information to its original form. As with any security method, there are both pluses and minuses to using data encryption: What if you forget the key or secret password? Worse yet, what if your computer or disk drive is stolen? Although it may take time, eventually, a competitor will probably be able to decode your encryption program.

Another method of data security is to back up an entire system on tape and then delete or reformat the hard disk. Unfortunately, this method isn't *very* secure as all sorts of "undelete" and "unformat" programs are available. Only a low-level format or a utility program such as *Norton's Wipedisk* will truly leave no trace of data.

Most anything you *do* with software, you can also *undo* with software, including data encryption, virus detection, and other security methods. The best way to safeguard against stolen data is to physically displace it—if the data isn't there, it can't be stolen. On the other hand, if it's on a file server (on a LAN), there's a chance it *can* be stolen.

Tape backup systems are really the best answer to virus, Trojan, and data security problems. *Back up your disks daily.* If you want no trace of information on your hard disk and if your backup software is capable, do a "mirror-image" backup, followed by a program such as *Norton's Wipedisk.* You may want to make two copies of your backup and put one in a safe deposit box or send it off to a remote storage site, possibly in another state.

For those who are really serious, you can write your own tape backup program to store the data in a way unfamiliar to others who use the same tape backup device. They'll lack the unique backup program you wrote that's necessary to interpret how the data is actually stored.

Since the floppy disk drive is a great way to introduce or take files from a computer, consider hardwiring the power to the disk drives via a physical key switch. The key would have to be in the *on* position to start the machine and then turned to *off* and removed once the machine is started, which would render the floppy drives inactive.

You can also either remove the serial port or rewire it so a special cable is needed to connect it to a modem. This insures no unauthorized data transfer via serial port. The parallel port can also be rewired so a special cable is needed to use the port (some file transfer programs use the parallel port to transfer data between machines). Anything allowing data going out of or coming into the computer can be rewired so special cables are needed (serial and parallel ports); or, you can break a vital connection to the port from inside and route the ends to a key switch.

Smaller Offices

Most small professional offices—for doctors, attorneys, accountants, and so on—are now automated, and while an office's employees may know how to use the company's database, spreadsheet, word processor, or billing system (and even how to use a tape or disk to make periodic backups), they actually know very little about computers.

In the professional offices I automate, each computer is set up with a simple password program that executes as soon the machine is turned on. The program won't allow anyone into the system without the correct password, and it logs both the date and time that password is entered. Also, different passwords are assigned to different people in order to keep track of who logs on and when. Simple programs such as format, back-up, and restore are renamed to cryptic names, and batch files replace these programs; these batch files ask for passwords and have the same name.

In other cases, a master program that asks for passwords and presents a menu of the vital programs—format, backup, restore, and others—must be started. The user chooses which program to run and the system then asks for the password. If the password entered is acceptable, the program (renamed to a cryptic name) is called to perform the task.

Editor's Note: Chuck Gilmore may be reached at Gilmore Systems, P.O. Box 3831, Beverly Hills, California 90212-0831, (213) 275-8006 voice, or (213) 276-5263 data. The latter number is an electronic bulletin board from which you can download demonstration versions of his programs.

7
COMPUTER VIRUSES

The popular press has been full lately of computer virus attack reports. Protecting your system from these destructive programs is very much a computer security concern.

Virus is a catchy term that conjures up memories (for those of us old enough to remember) of the polio epidemic in the early 1950s and we can all relate to the AIDS virus that is an international health concern today. Unfortunately, the computer industry, so far, does not have the sort of third-party organizations for testing and research—to say nothing of the dissemination of accurate information—that the medical community has long had in place.

We were afraid of polio, and we are afraid of AIDS. Thanks to Drs. Salk and Sabin, polio no longer threatens us. Millions and millions of research dollars are being spent in the battle against AIDS and many more millions are spent to care for its victims. Computer viruses cannot destroy life, but can destroy livelihood.

Much of the current interest in computer security has come about because of the media's enchantment with computer viruses. Magazines such as *Time* and *Business Week* have printed cover stories on the problem, television networks have produced features, and the daily and trade press have fanned the flames with lengthy, if not entirely accurate, coverage.

What Is a Virus?
If you are confused about viruses, you're not alone. Fifty industry experts gathered in New York last fall for a two-day symposium intended to reach "consensus" on various aspects of the

problem. The "best and the brightest" (as the group was styled by the sponsoring bodies) spent most of its time arguing over nomenclature.

The first mention of a computer virus was by a Ph.D. candidate at the University of Cincinnati, Fred Cohen, in his doctoral thesis. Cohen's theoretical definition has long been accepted by the scholarly community and has strong proponents among the "experts."

But a theoretical definition, however "on point" it may be, will not necessarily hold up as a working definition in an evolving field. A problem will often, as it has in the case of viruses, create its own definition, especially as "super mutant" forms develop. An originally clear definition may be muddied or even changed by popular misunderstanding and misuse.

A good "real world" example is the word *hopefully* which has come to mean "I hope" rather than remaining in its proper place as a useful adverb. If I were to say, "Hopefully you will read this book," I would probably mean, in the parlance of 1988, "I hope you will read this book." In days gone by, the intended meaning would have been more along the lines of, "Read this book with hope for it will answer your questions about computer security."

What, then, is the definition of a *virus*? The essential component of the definition of virus is the ability to either replicate or propagate its own string of code instructions, depending on the expert consulted. But the experts do agree that reproduction is essential to the definition, regardless of the chosen verb.

That said, let's consider the word "destruction." Some would (and have, with great vigor) argue that a virus can be *benign*—it only reproduces and does not destroy anything. But what about the space on a disk that the copy takes up? Has the user not lost the use of that space? It is destruction of resources if not actual data. So viruses cannot, by this definition, be benign.

What about the famous CHRISTMA.EXE "virus?" (The "Merry Christmas" message that zapped from one electronic mail directory to the next, addressed itself to everyone in the subsequent directory, and so on and so on.) According to

IBM's experts, CHRISTMA was not a virus as it did not *repli-cate.* Nevertheless, it brought one of the world's largest networks to a limping halt as available resources were chewed up. Destruction of resources—no replication. A fine tautological point.

Two thousand PCs at a huge corporation were taken out of service for almost 24 hours after a message appeared on a single word processing floppy disk which indicated a virus had been planted on a certain day and was due to "go off" 20 days hence. The message was found on the supposed nineteenth day. The security personnel took the only conservative step; they shut down the computers and consulting experts.

What did the experts find? A simple but very scary text file. No executable code at all. What appeared on the screen was this:

HELLO............... THIS IS A VIRUS ..... COURTESY OF YOUR FRIENDLY AT&T WORLD I ARRIVED AT YOUR COMPUTER VIA ANNUS - ADVANCED NANOSECOND NETWORK SYS-TEMS - VIRUS ORIGINATED IN NEW YORK, ON JAN 1, 1988, AT 4:33 AM. I GOTCHA ON 07. 30. 88. INCLUDING YOU, SO FAR I HAVE VISITED 298 INSTALLATIONS. I AM DESIGNED TO DO NO SERIOUS HARM FOR 20 DAYS;
THEN, ISSUE THIS MESSAGE AND BE DORMANT FOR 200 DAYS. HOPE YOU CAN FIND ME BY THEN, OTHER...WISE I BECOME NASTY. .... RTWDTW

Fortunately, the original disk was available for evaluation and the magic of overnight courier service made the down time as short as possible.

Experts' opinions aside, the corporation still had to begin the tedious process of checking for adequate backups, the presence of hidden or unknown files on every machine, and examining floppies for any other evidence. *Just to be safe.*

Was it simply someone's idea of fun to write such a message during a boring afternoon hour with no idea of the ultimate result—panic and confusion? Was it intended to bring productive work to a halt? Or maybe the experts missed something and all 2000 computers will vaporize at some yet unknown date in the future. Did it replicate? No. Did it destroy data? No. Did it destroy resources? A fine point, again. There were 2000 PCs out of service for 24 hours and the technical personnel's time for security checking was surely costly to the corporation.

Fear and Confusion

As we have suggested several times before, computer users in the late 1980s are disposed to see viruses lurking behind every error message that appears on the screen. While we favor awareness, this paranoia has become a costly factor in computer operations.

At Panda Systems, a large number of live viruses are held in captivity with extremely stringent security precautions in place at all times. Nevertheless, an unexplained error message can cause complete staff panic. The author was examining a commercial floppy disk offering antivirus utilities downloaded from bulletin boards when a program known to have been "hacked" into a virus on several occasions appeared in the DIR listing. "Clean" procedures and disaster prevention utilities in place, we carefully looked into the program's code; nothing appeared to be amiss.

Later the same day, the disk was loaded to print a directory to accompany the staff notes on the product. The DIR showed entry after entry called DEMO1", DEMO2", and so forth, four hidden files, three files with unrecognizable names and ZERO bytes free! Panic? Yes, indeed. The answer was simple. The vendor has also provided *another* disk demonstrating a different product with *exactly the same label*. Time lost: only four person-hours. Destruction of resources? We thought so.

One source has reported, as part of a set of statistics on the issue, that 94 percent of problems examined were *not* "viruses." *But* 30 percent of those looked at were bombs, Trojan horses, or other destructive code. A little quick math indicates that one-third of the incidents analyzed included the element of *data destruction*. (Author's note: These "statistics" are unsubstantiated in the traditional research sense and represent only the findings of a single entity. Further, the organization states it was unable to analyze almost half the evidence presented to them. Panda Systems has found the occurrence of destructive code, virus or otherwise, in suspected "incidents" to be closer to 75 percent.)

It's probably best to leave such semantic debates to the scholars and try to consider viruses as part of the greater question of computer security which *must* include the issue of destructive code and destruction of resources.

The Birth of a Virus

Let's attend the birth of a virus. The midwife is a programmer with a modicum of skill and an antisocial bent. A handy little utility that has enjoyed good public acceptance is downloaded from a bulletin board by the midwife and placed in the *in vitro* medium—the PC. A "quick hack," maybe only the simple insertion of the instruction FORMAT C: so the first execution of the utility would perform a logical format of the default hard drive, is all that's needed. The new creation is loaded back on the bulletin board (the clever programmer has made sure that the file size and file date are the same as the original ...) and sets out to make a name for itself—and its creator—in the PC world.

A more complex instruction set might include hiding a new destructive program on a hard drive that would silently copy itself and another destructive program to every floppy accessed by the system and, after 25 such copies, would "blow up" and destroy the hard drive and itself. The possibilities are limited only by the skill and malice of the programmer/midwife.

Enter the user. You've heard from associates that there is a super utility called COSMIC.EXE that does *everything* you ever wanted a utility to do and it's *free*. Just download it from any bulletin board. You download the program and take a quick look, WOW! Just as advertised! (But with a few unadvertised features—this is the more complex "hack" described above.) You copy the file to the DOS/UTIL subdirectory where you keep all your goodies. The play begins.

Act One, Scene Two: Tomorrow morning, 8:00 a.m. Full of pride in your new discovery, you demonstrate the new acquisition to three or four co-workers on *their* machines. You're a hero!

Act One, Scene Three: That night, at home. A good portion of your productive work day was wasted demonstrating COSMIC to your pals; the spreadsheet the boss wanted tomorrow isn't done. You've brought it home. Pop the work floppy in A:, finalize the numbers, and put it back in your briefcase. Travelling along with the spreadsheet is a little something extra. (It's a good thing it didn't take too long because your son needs the computer to copy a game to take next door to his friend whose mom is the MIS manager of a large bank and is working at home tonight, too.)

Act Two, Scene One: The next day, 7:45 a.m. You go in early to impress the boss with your promptness and dedication and report to his office. He reviews the spreadsheet after copying it to his PC and pronounces it good. You return the work disk to your secretary (since it contains the report that needs to go to the typing pool) and the boss accesses the 500 node executive LAN to report on progress to *his* boss.

The rest of this play can be written in the reader's imagination. How far has our newborn travelled in the first 36 hours of its life before issuing its first cry? How far will it travel—from individual machine to another individual machine, along the LAN, into the typing pool that handles hundreds of floppy disks daily, to another company—before the sun sets today? And when will the curtain fall?

The stuff of science fiction? No. This is the stuff of harsh reality. To too many users, individual or corporate, such a scenario is often too terrifying to even consider, much less guard against.

What if COSMIC were only a Trojan horse, programmed to go to work the minute COSMIC was entered at the keyboard? The loss could have been limited to *only* everything on the user's hard drive—and maybe *only* for a relatively brief time in the grander scheme of things as there are commercial utilities available to recover from a mistaken logical format. But *what if* the tiny code segment the midwife included performed a *virtual* (FDISK) format of the default drive? Or scrambled the boot sector? Or destroyed the File Allocation Table (FAT)? Again, the reader's imagination can take over.

A Conspiracy of Silence?

The security industry has stated absolutely, "The potential for damage from destructive code/viruses is *unlimited*."

Returning to the *conspiracy of silence* idea presented earlier in this book, the authors, while on deadline, learned of the Marijuana Virus. Unbeknownst to the international security community, this virus had been cropping up in Australia and New Zealand for over one and a half years. Supposedly a simple (benign?) message such as "Legalize Marijuana," appearing at random, was its original form. The report indicates that the program was later hacked into truly destructive code. A victim of the destructive form, a bank, went public with the information—a rare occurrence, indeed. Immediately upon the bank's open release of this information, other reports came flooding in.

The conspiracy of silence has now progressed from the manufacturers and salespeople, who don't want purchasers/users to know, to the purchasers/users who don't want the purchasers/users of *their* services to know! Add in the personal pride of the security "experts" who don't want their industry colleagues to know what is known to them, lest their expert status be compromised—it all conspires to keep *you* in the dark about what's *really* happening.

There is a strong conviction in the industry that an "It can't happen to me," mentality is at large and most users, individual or corporate, will not recognize the problem—or admit to their fears—until *they* are victimized. Then the bind doubles: Faced with the possibility of admitting they were either stupid or unaware, the silence deepens.

One of the most famous stories on the virus circuit—and one which may have been enhanced considerably in the telling—is this:

An antivirus product vendor received a panic call requesting 10 (or 20, or 30, or 100) copies of its virus killer software NOW! The "ship to" location alerted the vendor that the purchaser represented an extremely major player in the computer industry. The story continues to include the vendor's discovery that the purchaser's manufacturing facility had received a "bomb threat": "All your computers will go down on Friday!"

The company turned off every computer on the entire site and went on a search for the bomb. Was it found? The story does not go that far.

It Can't Happen to Me

We all remember the famous story that has become part of our rich oral tradition of the rat in the soda/beer bottle that someone supposedly found (and sued the soda/beer company for millions). Is this story made of the same stuff? We'll probably never know. But there is a lesson to be learned. No one would ever risk human life in the face of a bomb threat by failing to evacuate a building, but thousands and thousands of individuals and managers daily turn their collective back on the clearly stated threat against the lifeblood of their operations. This lifeblood is data.

Every user knows the cold sweat feeling that immediately follows an egregious error—especially one that could have been prevented with a little more thought and care. In the ensuing panic, the lively human mind often turns quickly to either a way to repair the damage *or* blame it on someone or something else. Every manager knows the frustration of dealing with the user who anthropomorphises the PC at every turn and whines, "*It* won't let me . . . ." How many people are confident enough to admit to their limitations and mistakes? How much data—or any other things of value—have been lost through questions unasked and errors left hanging in silence?

Everyone knows the simple and elemental human reaction when faced with a concept whose enormity is just *too much*—turn away and don't think about it. And the wonderful machine known as the human mind is all too willing to aid and abet this process. "I'll think about it tomorrow. Tomorrow is another day." Thank you, Scarlett O'Hara.

If this chapter does nothing else, it is the authors' sincere hope that each and every reader will understand the *clear and present danger* to data, to day to day operations, to the very machines entrusted with our own essence, and to the profitability of the company. Fear can only be fought with knowledge.

8
THIEVES IN THREE-PIECE SUITS

Several years ago, a popular book on dressing for success stated that a man in "the uniform" of a 3-piece suit and a khaki colored raincoat could "borrow" money for train fare far more frequently than *the same man* dressed in a less "acceptable" manner—which was the simple replacement of the khaki raincoat with a black one.

Experience tells us that "uniforms" inspire confidence, trust, respect and (even more interestingly) *the desire to win the approval of the wearer of the uniform.* One of the authors conducted an informal experiment along the same lines. When she dressed in the traditional "uniform"—gray flannel suit, starched shirt and yellow foulard tie, simple gold earrings and Timex watch, she was treated as an *equal* by prospective clients, including lunch in the company cafeteria. When she donned a silk designer dress, a Rolex watch, diamond earrings and put the emerald engagement ring back on her finger, lunch was *always* at the best restaurants and her contact's "boss" was *always* asked to attend planning conferences.

Appearances Can Be Deceiving

The same author, working on the office automation startup of an international law firm's new Los Angeles office, had come in before business hours one morning to "tweak" the PCs in the word processing center. Her plans included a three-mile run before reappearing as "The Consultant," so her costume was a

sweatsuit and a "do rag" around her curly hair—rather standard attire for word processing center employees in LA. An extremely anxious young attorney, hoping to make partner as soon
as possible by virtue of diligence and a supremely bad attitude,
burst into the word processing center and *demanded* that his
overnight work miracles be word processed immediately.

There was no argument to be brooked. After all, work had
to be done and there was no one else to do it. And a young attorney's hubris knows no bounds. The hand-written pages were
deciphered, typed, formatted, printed, and carried into the
young man's office.

Dismissed with a glary stare and a curt, "Just leave it!"
our heroine chose not to yield the field and simply stated to the
attorney, "Mr. Foolscape, you just paid $1000 for that typing
and put the word processing center automation project at least
one day behind. I hope it was worth it." Never was an early
morning run more welcome. The young attorney was soon
gone from the big international law firm where he had planned
to find fame and fortune. Was it the sweatsuit, the "do rag"
and the misconceptions associated with attire that contributed
to his downfall? Possibly.

The negative jokes surrounding the legal profession can
just as easily be translated to incisive commentary on consultants. Their numbers are legion and they come in all sizes,
shapes and flavors. While we all need expert advice from time
to time and there is much to be said for being bright enough to
buy a wheel instead of trying to reinvent one, we all too often
open our wallets along with our requests for help and assistance.

With these stories in mind, let's consider what happens
when we invite "experts" (be they consultants, technical support people, or repair crews) into our offices and *our data*.

A License to Steal

Going back to one of the recurring themes in this book, the
fear of admitting to a lack of knowledge, it's clear that failing to
ask questions or gather knowledge is tantamount to giving
away a license to steal. In comes the consultant with a $50
haircut and a $400 suit and begins to speak in a jargon few un-
derstand. Immediately we are at the mercy of our pride and the

larcenous bent of those who would exploit it.

A case in point is that of a small law office with three attorneys who decided to computerize their billing. Gathering information from advertising in legal journals, they called several vendors of billing packages that appeared to meet their needs and desires. After listening to, and pretending to understand, each vendor's sales pitch, they selected one. Their ultimate criterion was the "turn key" approach offered. The PC would be brought into the office, the billing software already installed, and their billing clerk would be trained by the "experts." Smooth sailing.

Three months and four billing clerks later, the firm's bills were still being produced on typewriters and over $20,000 worth of hardware and software were gathering dust. The system was almost impossible to operate, was far more tedious than manual billing, and the software routinely froze the computer, losing all new data entries. Even worse, the system only printed on old-fashioned green-line type paper and the resulting invoices were not in keeping with the firm's image of itself.

A long-time friend of one of the attorneys, who was a computer specialist, stopped in the office late one afternoon to inquire about the possibility of a quick after-work drink and a catchup on local gossip.

"Would you mind," inquired the attorney in his kindest way, "looking at our new computer?"

"New computer? Sure."

The look disclosed an IBM PC/AT—very new (and expensive) technology at that time—bound, chained and gagged as a prisoner to the vendor's proprietary billing system. The mare's nest of programming bypassing DOS and the tangled web of user instructions and menu structures rendered the specialist almost speechless.

"How much did you pay for this [expletive deleted]?"

The attorney silently passed over the contract file. The firm had obligated itself to pay the vendor thousands and thousands of dollars in *lease payments* over the three-year life of the contract and would have the right to *purchase* the hardware *only* at the end of the three year term. At full retail. With the specialist's assistance, the firm finally prevailed upon the vendor to cancel the agreement and take back the equipment. The

85

lease payments already made were lost, the time setting up the firm's billing information on the shoddy system was lost, the confidence of the attorneys and their staff in computers and the honesty of "specialists" was shaken.

Why didn't the attorney ask his friend, a true specialist with no products to shill? Embarrassment at his lack of knowledge?

Guidelines for Your Own Protection

Three professional groups, all of which depend almost entirely on the proper and timely billing of time expended for their income and profit, are among the traditional targets for this sort of thievery. Members of each profession are easily identified and marketing can be heavily targeting and specialized. The three: lawyers, doctors, and accountants.

While John or Jane Doe might spend several weeks or months reading computer books and magazines, visiting computer stores, collecting references, and talking with friends about a prospective purchase, many professionals are unwilling to take billable time away from their practices for such research and are often unwilling to disclose to colleagues or competitors their lack of either knowledge or technology. So they turn to another "professional," often with disastrous results.

There are a few simple guidelines for *everyone* to follow in order that assets—time and money—be preserved and that a finished product is *really* what's wanted.

Know what you want. This does not mean that you should have to come up with technical specifications for each and every chip bank but, rather, what you want to *do* with a computer system. The conversion process from a manual system (billing, inventory tracking, client management, whatever) to one which is automated by computers is not at all mysterious. If client records are now being kept in a card file, and the cards are printed to your specifications, it's not hard to imagine (or program) the same form on a computer screen.

If you want *more,* have some idea of what that is. *But* the first step is evaluating what you're currently doing by hand and getting that programmed and in place. Once the power of the automated system is appreciated, "more" is easy to add.

Know the difference between *custom* **and** *off-the-shelf* **programs.** A custom program is written *exactly* to your specifications. Off-the-shelf products must be written to appeal to a wide variety of users and may not include *exactly* what you want or need. There may be features that you will never use, or features missing that will require a serious change in your business practices.

Know the difference between a *consultant* **and a** *sales consultant.* One makes his or her daily bread through knowledge, expertise, and the ability to evaluate your unique situation and offer sound professional advice for your consideration and decision-making processes. The latter takes orders. A professional consultant with no other product to sell but time and experience may charge as little as $40 per hour or as much as $200. Sales consultants' "professional fees" are built into the cost of the products they sell.

Do some research, but don't reinvent the wheel. Know enough that you're familiar with the basic vocabulary and don't be afraid to step in and ask for definitions or explanations of jargon and bafflegab. Most true consultants list *service and education* as their most important functional priorities.

Software comes first. Form follows function. This goes back to *knowing what you want.* A $12,000 laser printer capable of producing 20 pages a minute is a great sale for the vendor but not too useful outside a huge word processing center where "throughput" is the key to success. *And,* in that huge word processing center, such a printer would most likely service several workstations. On the other hand, a $2,000 laser printer may be an *absolute necessity* for the small business that depends upon the professional quality of correspondence, proposals, or reports to build an image.

Do you *really* need the latest and greatest PC? Or could your work be done on a slower and less expensive system? The authors' collective stomach churns slightly at the recollection of a "consultant" who convinced a client that its work could *only* be done efficiently *if* an expensive minicomputer was part of the original installation.

The mini had to be custom-made by the consultant's firm, featured a bizarre operating system known only to a select few and would have required a full-time system manager to keep things straight. There is, however, some form of justice in the world: The mini could not be delivered in time for the client's startup and, when it was finally ready to go, several months later, the client's work was progressing so well *just on PCs* that the mini may still be gathering dust on the tech bench. But it was *essential*.

Beware the VAR and VAD (Value-Added Retailer and Value-Added Dealer). The Vs are bundling hardware and software together and often taking a cut on both. Always ask for the separate component prices to be broken out. *Then* shop around. If the vendor is unwilling to provide such a breakout, *run.*

Don't be afraid to "cherry pick." This is a pejorative term applied by computer stores to the buyer who would shop on price, buying one item here, one item there. The larger your "buy," the more you can save. With the wealth of mail-order suppliers offering hardware and software at prices barely above wholesale, a prospective purchaser can have a field day shaving a dollar here, three dollars another place. Be wary of that kind of "cherry picking," it will make you crazy.

Visit the cherry orchard *only* after some reputation checking. There are mail order companies which have long been in business and have fine reputations. Other mail order companies have been in business only long enough to purchase their two-page ad in a computer magazine, have no inventory and only the desire to make a quick buck. Many mail order houses have complete technical phone support and liberal return policies as well as very competitive prices.

Be leary of any "deal" that ties you in to a single consultant, vendor, operating system, programming language, or service organization. Service contracts are a good example: "If we don't service it (at $100 a year for the contract), we won't guarantee it." Jan Diamondstone of Interactive Design, Inc. represents an interesting new wave of professional thinking on service contracts. "The technology is so reliable and inexpensive now it's cheaper to throw one PC away every year than keep up service contracts." Jan hasn't thrown a PC out yet but keeps daily backups and a spare machine available.

**If you purchase "custom" programming, make sure you
lock in the programmer/vendor with an escrow of the source
(original) code in a safe location.** Should the programmer die,
retire to the South of France on the profits from your project,
or otherwise become unavailable to you, you *must* have access
to the underlying work or your system will become useless if it
cannot grow.

If you purchase off-the-shelf software, *make sure* you know
what form the stored data will take. If, for example, billing data
cannot be accessed for a general ledger or additional reports, it
will either be lost for those purposes or require a duplication of
data entry. Some extremely clever off-the-shelf programming
thieves will offer to write additional reports to suit a client's
purposes at costs approximating those of launching a space
shuttle.

Theft of Resources

So far, we have looked at theft of financial resources through
misrepresentation, soft fraud, and preying on the consumer's
self-inflicted lack of knowledge. Let's now turn to the theft of
owned resources.

An interesting point of view was offered by a physician
friend who had almost finished reading a very expensive and
highly regarded book. When asked if the book could be bor-
rowed when he was finished, his startling response was, "You
can afford to buy a copy. The book is so excellent that the author and the publisher deserve every penny!" Clearly, copyright
laws do not prohibit a book from being loaned—libraries do it
all the time. And the copyright laws that apply to computer
software are often compared to those for other published
works—books in particular.

Why, then, do otherwise respectable citizens who would
never consider photocopying a best-seller to add to their personal library, copy software for their collection? It's quicker to
copy software, costs less, and a pirated backup/working copy
looks the same as one made legitimately. And the chances of
legal representatives of a major software developer entering
one's home office with the appropriate legal documents to

search for unauthorized copies are roughly about the same as Victor Hugo making a surprise appearance to seek photocopies of *Les Miserables.*

Shareware

But what about freeware/shareware. Thousands upon thousands of programs are available at the cost of a telephone connection to users of bulletin boards and on-line services. These programs represent the creativity and hard work of some extremely talented people. Most are useful, many are very good, some are excellent, a few have become *industry standards.* Without exception that we have seen, the writer includes a request to evaluate the software and, if it is found useful, requests a token payment. The writer's name, address, and phone number are included with the documentation. (If it is not, *do not* use it! Never use a program you can't check with the writer or publisher.)

At a recent meeting of PC users in a large city, several questions were asked of those attending. Two are noteworthy for our purposes: Less than 5 percent of those attending had backed up in the past 30 days; 100 percent were using at least one shareware program without making the token payment to the author.

Andy Hopkins, Vice President for Development of Panda Systems, and author of the chapter on technical considerations earlier in this book, wrote two small programs in 1985: CHK4BOMB and BOMSQAD. These programs are considered by many industry experts to be the beginning of the anti-destructive code genre of programming. Almost *every* book or article on the virus problem has included these programs. There are two sad parts to this story, one for some users, the other for Andy.

Originally written for his local PC users' group bulletin board to check for Trojan horses, the programs were "loaned" by the caring SYSOP to other BBS SYSOPS. Somehow the programs filtered onto the bulletin boards themselves and became so widely distributed that *LOTUS Magazine* featured them in a July 1986 article on Trojan Horses (viruses weren't getting any press at that time). Time passed, the programs were passed into more and more hands. They became *industry standards*. Though basically "quick hacks" and containing a few minor errors, these programs did what they were intended to do and did it well. (What more could anyone ask?)

Sad part #1: Several ingenious programmers decided to hide a killer in the cure, and "hacked" versions, including destructive code, began to appear in late 1987. Though Andy's name and address were prominently displayed, no user *ever* called unless he/she had happened to pick up one of the "improved" versions and had suffered a severe loss of resources.

Sad Part #2: In the three years since these programs were written, Andy estimates he has received *less than* $500 from the thousands of people estimated to be using the programs. National consulting organizations currently distribute them as part of utility packages to clients, and vendors are now *selling* them, some without bothering to remove the "all rights reserved" statement from the on-disk documentation.

Another antivirus software author, Ross Greenberg, was chagrined to discover that one of the early versions of his FLU_SHOT program had also been adjusted to include destructive code. He immediately issued a new release with strong caveats to the user. Taking a further hard line, Ross refuses technical support on virus issues to users who *have not registered* the product. As an interesting wrinkle, Ross allows the registration fee check to be made payable to a charity of the user's choice.

The point about shareware to be made and understood is: the thief in the three piece suit *may be you!*

Copyrights

Let's move now to some more obvious, and prosecutable, forms of theft.

Every consultant knows the experience of a client who cannot understand why a single copy of software, often very expensive software, cannot be used on more than one machine. Some of the most obdurate in their refusal to understand are professionals whose livelihood depends on their own work product. The most careful, not surprisingly, are companies who depend heavily on the protection offered to them by their proprietary patents, copyrights, and trademarks. The larger the company, the more careful.

A senior partner in a small but prestigious lawfirm was dragged, kicking and screaming, into the age of automation. Three years' of his "forgotten" invoices were promptly handled by the new computer's billing system, his personal partnerhip share was higher than ever before, *and* he showed a remarkable understanding of the benefits, hows, and whys of computers. His secretary was the first in the office to have her own PC for word processing. Another PC for his two paralegals was quickly added and he had a client management system custom programmed for the state-of-the-art hot PC that soon appeared on *his own desk*.

Enjoying his status as "sultan of silicon" in the office, he requested that all his personal billing be moved into his own empire and *then* fed into the general ledger system. The software could do it, right? Right. But you must purchase another copy of the software at $1,500. No, the firm *owns* the software. No, the firm has *licensed one copy* of the software. The ensuing back-and-forth between the attorney and the firm's consultant ended with the consultant's final advice to the client: that he seek professional assistance, both on automation and copyright matters, elsewhere.

Pilferage

We once watched, in the "camouflage" costume of a simple office employee working late, a technician enter a client firm to replace a toner cartridge in a laser printer. The job took three minutes. The "techie" then walked directly to the closet where supplies were stored and proceeded to "shop."

Among the goodies available were original *shrink wrapped* software packages, floppy disks and manuals, for thousands of dollars worth of PC software in many multiples of each (each PC requires an individual copy of each software program under normal licensing agreements—usually a single package is used for installation). The techie selected one of each (and tucked a package of pens in his pocket for good measure), closed the cabinet, and began to saunter away. He did not get away with it that time.

Can we imagine anyone who might encourage technical employees to carry away "new" software that could then be resold at full price to a second (or third) customer?

What about the tech type whose secret desire is to become a "programmer/consultant" and knows about the new project under development that's being tested? The code is still raw (not compiled or encrypted) and therefore available for examination and learning. A quick copy to those preformatted disks steals the work product of the writers with whom our techie will soon be competing based on stolen knowledge.

Another version of the same story would be two competing departments in the same company. One department begins development of a PC-based system to do what's been done by hand—in both departments, just for different products—for far too long. Human nature being what it is, the manager developing the new system brags a little too much at the divisional golf outing. The other manager *just might* be PC-literate, or has a subordinate who is, and they are both headed for the fast track. A little internal espionage and the fast-tracking manager *might* have *his* new system in place first.

Conclusions

These may seem to be minor "hits" in the world of computer crime. The giants are already rich, any custom developer who's foolish enough to put raw code on a test machine deserves to have it stolen and the whole underlying philosophy of PCs is the free and open exchange of information, right? But what if it's your data that's gone?

A major spokesperson for the computer security industry tells, after the caveat that the tale may be part of the emerging security apocrypha, of a government agency whose security precautions were of the highest and tightest—until a computer got sick one day. The entire system unit, complete with megabytes of highly secure data, was sent out to a local computer store for repair. What if the repairman worked for the KGB, or just the competition seeking to steal a juicy contract plumb?

Let's spin this one just a little further; your competition *knows* you are working on ABC or XYZ project. Gaining access to your data or working methods will give them a total competitive edge. Some quiet research by the enemy will soon glean who's doing your tech support, or who provides your temporary office help. How simple for them to place a trusted employee, with a desire for advancement and a talent for espionage, on your site. If you are worrying, you should be.

The *prevention* side of these issues will be covered in greater detail in the chapter on security planning. But in the meantime, make sure *you* are not, whether by design or ignorance, a member of the thief brigade.

9
COMMUNICATION AND NETWORK SECURITY

Invisible webs spin across the face of the world, each strand vibrating with the transmission of data. Local area networks—statewide, nationwide, and worldwide—tie many thousands of computers firmly together. Transmitted data is the lifeblood of commerce, research, and government. Yet, there exist those who stalk the webs and would suck this blood like spiders, leaving behind only the dry husks of their victims. Whether interference with networked computers is malicious or not, communications security is important, and that's what this chapter discusses.

Chuck Forsberg—author of the popular Ymodem and Zmodem communications protocols, and of the Zcomm and Pro-Yam modem programs—puts it well. "With communications," he said, "if anything can happen, it probably will. Or at least it will happen to your neighbor."

Telephones, an Often Unguarded Door

Rent-a-cops can valiantly protect offices at night. If they're good and don't fall asleep or drink or smoke "ginja weed" on the job, chances are no one is going to physically break into a particular computer system. But, of course, most offices have a type of door now that's left unlocked and unguarded 24 hours a day, seven days a week. This "door" is the telephone!

When a computer answers the phone, no one can see who's on the other end, or know where they are. If the password is correct, the computer connects and bares its soul. The

person on the other end could be a legitimate company salesman in a Holiday Inn in Dubuque, Iowa using a laptop personal computer to call in the day's orders, or a hacker in West
Germany intent on playing hopscotch through the system (as
the Department of Defense found out the hard way in 1987).

Disconnecting the phone line overnight is no answer. In
the Information Age it's almost absolutely imperative that
computers be able to communicate constantly. Many automatic
processes can be done at night, using the cheaper long distance
and packet network charges. Customers can call in orders even
when no one is in the office. Telecommunication is now a necessity, but so too are the security protocols to protect the system at this, its weakest point.

Security packages now present in most of the larger mainframe systems make breaking into those types of computers
more difficult (although by no means impossible). The various
commercial packages available offer sophisticated password
and PIN (Personal Identification Numbers, also sometimes
called *usernames)*. They also implement "data classification."

Data classification is the process by which access for various users can be controlled. The MIS person in charge of security can designate which files or parts of files an individual
user can access, and what operations they can instruct the host
computer to perform. Security, by these methods, can be applied in "layers," and the more sensitive information can be
compartmentalized.

Here's a quick analogy. If you walk into a shoe store
downtown during business hours, you can go through the front
door because, as a potential customer, the door is unlocked for
you. But the stockroom is off limits as is the manager's office
and *certainly* the safe. A clerk in this store, however, can go
into the stockroom whenever necessary, and even into the
manager's office under more controlled conditions. He or she,
however, is not allowed to open the safe. The manager has the
highest level of access; she can open the safe, take out the
checkbook, and write a check for a C.O.D. delivery. This is a
rough approximation of layered access on a computer system.

Naturally, any security system has weak points. If there's a
large crowd and only a few clerks, an unauthorized person

could sneak into the stockroom. He could then unlock the back door and pass out stacks of shoeboxes to an accomplice. Crimes like this happen constantly in the retail world, and analogous crimes happen constantly in the data processing world.

If the computer system is "online," that is, connected to the telephone lines, security is even worse. At night, no one is in the shoe store. What if the front door had not a key lock, but one activated by a keypad, like the touchtone pad on most telephones? Anyone who was willing to try enough combinations could open the door and walk in. This intruder could then find his way through the dark store to the stockroom and pick out whatever he could carry away. Or he could enter the manager's office and attempt to open the safe.

Since people breaking into a computer system over the phone lines have their own computers (it is, after all, a computer-to-computer medium), the task of finding the proper access codes is simplified. If nothing stops these phreakers, as they call themselves, their computers can try thousands of possible combinations in an incredibly short time.

Don't Underestimate the Kids

Phreakers are not all kids, of course. Yet their sense of moral values is immature. Stealing information differs little from stealing hubcaps, other than it's indoor work and no heavy lifting is involved.

Any company, institution, or agency that has a computer connected to a telephone line is fair game. Clifford Stoll—in his article "Stalking the Wiley Hacker" for the May 1988 *Communications of the ACM*—relates the antics of a West German hacker. This person invaded literally dozens of computer systems over the course of a year, including many in the United States.

He was eventually caught when legitimate computer users at Berkeley, California saw him on their system and called in various authorities—eventually including those authorities in West Germany where the hacker was physically located. This particular intruder was obviously searching for military-related information.

He was able to exploit certain weaknesses in the Unix operating system, and waltz unseen and unmolested around a network of hundreds of computers all over the world. Similar security "holes" allowed the massive "virus" attack of November 4, 1988, which shut down over 6,000 computers on the Defense Department-sponsored Arpanet at such places as M.I.T, Harvard, Stanford University, Lawrence Livermore Labs, and NASA's Ames Research Laboratory.

Mr. Stoll concludes in his article that the perpetrator needed only a modicum of knowledge of the network's weaknesses, and a lot of persistence. An astounding 13 percent of these supposedly secure computers gave the hacker information about themselves, 5 percent let him log on and access data, and 2 percent *gave him system-manager privileges!*

One fact that helps hackers tremendously is the "commonality" of passwords. A lot of passwords are popular—that is, many different users tend to think of them because they're easy to remember. A phreaker needs merely to have a dictionary file of such widely-used passwords and let his computer try them until one works.

The "virus" mentioned above which attacked Arpanet on November 4, 1988 made use of this incredible security lapse also. Actually, by the way, according to computer experts, this intruding program was really a *worm* instead of a virus, the difference being that a virus can infect other programs, whereas this one simply got into the system and made copies of itself until memory was filled up.

The worm program had available a large file of common passwords and just kept trying, at computer speed, until one of the passwords worked; then the program could log onto the system being attacked. Copies of the worm also started working, and soon over 6,000 computers were "infected."

It's natural that using computers and reading science fiction goes hand-in-hand. One password often used (and found in the worm's password file), is "heinlein," after the late Robert A. Heinlein, the "Dean of Science Fiction." Another is "lazarus," from Heinlein's seminal character, Lazarus Long. Other passwords include "orwell," "snoopy," "aaa," "susan," "pam," "johnny," "kermit," and a whole raft of other first names.

Such passwords are easy to remember, right enough, but they also make a phreaker's task of breaking into a system much easier. Use a random combination of letters and numbers for passwords, the more random the better. We'll look at this in the next chapter, along with encryption techniques.

How Phreakers Break into *Your* System

To implement effective communications security, it's necessary to first understand some of the ways hackers and phreakers can rape a system. Such techniques are widely disseminated on underground "pirate" computer bulletin boards, and hackers read such publications as *2600* magazine to keep in touch with each other, and to gain knowledge.

Anyone interested in knowing more about computer phreaking can buy several publications on the subject, including *Computer Phreaking* and *Computer Phreaking Addendum* from Consumertronics (2011 Crescent Drive, P.O. Drawer 537, Alamogordo, NM 88310). These booklets, as is stressed numerous places within, are sold "for education purposes only."

This same company sells similar booklets on secret and survival radio, combat and survival weight fitness, credit card scams, stealth technology, cryptanalysis techniques, and ways of beating automatic teller machines.

John J. Williams, president of Comsumertronics, defends his publications. "Whenever controversial information is published," he said, "there is always some danger that it will be abused. That danger must be weighed against the people's right to know."

While corporate computer security executives may have heart attacks at some of the information published in these booklets, the point to be made here is that the same data is widely available to phreakers. You cannot stop the spread of it; you can only defend your system as resources allow.

Mr. Williams, in *Computer Phreaking Addendum,* details the various techniques phreakers use to penetrate systems. The first step, naturally, is to find out the system's phone number.

It's an indictment of today's lackadaisical concern with security that many of these numbers are simply listed in the phone book. A lot of companies aren't familiar enough with telephone company procedure to realize that their modem numbers are made public, while others subscribe to false economy and decide not to pay the extra for unlisted numbers.

Those companies that do pay extra for unlisted modem numbers many times do not get their money's worth. Large companies or institutions usually are assigned contiguous blocks of numbers. A phreaker examining the listing in the phone book can assume the missing numbers in the sequence make up those numbers that have modems and computers attached. Bingo, he's into your system!

Even if modem numbers are unlisted and are not obvious, numerous ways exist for phreakers to obtain them. This is called, in their parlance, "social engineering," and involves such methods as cultivating a friend at the phone company, or duping employees into thinking the phreaker is a fellow employee who legitimately needs the information. Once the number(s) is in a phreaker's hands, it's usually shared with others by being posted on underground computer bulletin boards. So, even if one phreaker is unable to break into a particular system, his friends can try it as well.

Should the phone book prove barren and social engineering fail, there are programs called "demon dialers" or "wargame dialers." These programs allow the phreaker's computer to go through a telephone exchange, calling one number after another and recording the ones that answer with a modem carrier (a high-pitched tone). Have you ever had *your* phone ring once or twice, but no one was there when you answered? The "demon dialers" are looking only for computers; they disconnect if a human picks up.

Demon dialing, of course, does not catch a system that may be connected at the time of the call (and thus be putting out a busy signal), but a determined phreaker can run through the exchange several times, at differing hours. Since this is an automatic process, his computer can be doing it while he's in class, or working at the car wash.

Once a system is found that the phreaker wants to penetrate, the fun begins. Some systems are incredibly simple because people, as we talked about above, use popular passwords. In the past (and we hope this practice is dying out fast), many just used "password" or "secret." These are easy enough to remember—for everyone!

In *Computer Phreaking Addendum*, Williams categorizes system penetration into four general methods: classic penetration, gathering intelligence, wiretapping, and Tempest-related methods.

Classic penetration involves a good deal of guessing, whether by the hacker or his computer. It's often made easy, and let us stress this again, by the use of popular passwords. Usually, once the phreaker can guess an account name and a password, he has pretty much free run of the system.

Intelligence gathering simply means obtaining accounts and passwords by such mundane means as going through a company's trash (companies have given away literally millions of dollars by leaving themselves open this way), or by duping company employees into divulging information that they should keep their lips zipped on.

Wiretapping is sometimes employed when the phreaker (or more likely computer criminal) is after a big score. This requires physical access to the phone lines connecting to a company or agency's computers. When such a tap is achieved, it's no problem to get user accounts and passwords. Just by recording all the regular logons for a day or so will give the phreaker scores if not hundreds of legitimate accounts and passwords.

Tempest methods (also known as Van Eyk Phreaking) gets its name from "tempest," the U.S. Government code word referring to "hardened" computers (those that don't radiate information). Since dozens of companies in engineering journals and computer magazines are advertising "tempest" machines, it's not exactly a secret any more.

Wim van Eyk, in a sanctioned experiment, first developed the techniques for eavesdropping on computers by using radios. Most of us know computers operate at such fast speeds as 10, 12, 16, or 20 megahertz per second. These particular frequencies, and others, are in the radio frequency spectrum (the ones given are all HF, or high frequency—the "short wave" of short wave radios). Faster computers are up in the VHF range.

Most of us also know that the Federal Communications Commission must approve a personal computer before it can be marketed in the United States. The reason is simple; because they're operating at radio frequencies, computers are also *transmitters.* So, just like the ham radio operator next door, the FCC wants to make sure the radio emissions from a computer are not strong enough to interfere with television sets and other legitimate, licensed, radio receivers.

A phreaker, a computer criminal, or an intelligence agent—if they get can close enough with the right equipment—can monitor what's going on in most current computers. A van parked down on the street could be recording access codes, or information directly from a computer as it operates.

Since Tempest-quality computers are still very expensive, there's not a lot you can use to protect yourself, other than metal cases, good shielding, and a nice solid earth ground. Luckily, Van Eyk techniques require sophistication and expensive efforts that most phreakers aren't going to make.

The prime line of defense you need to erect is against "classic" penetration techniques. Changing passwords, using passwords that don't lend themselves to guessing and, most importantly, instilling a sense of security in the average system user.

In the next chapter, we'll take a look at some specific ways communications security can be implemented.

Inside Calls

Phreakers, of course, aren't the only ones attempting to break into computer systems. Their antics are usually closer to juvenile high spirits than the destructive or larcenous intent of older computer criminals—who are often "insiders" such as employees or former employees of the company being robbed. We certainly do not endorse phreaker activities, but we do point out that the reason they do such things is because such things are generally *easy* to do. Computer security has a long way to go yet.

The problems of security are even worse when a company's employees are considered. After all, insiders do tend to pick up information, and among any group are those who may, under various circumstances, prove weak. Added to the lackadaisical attitude toward security protocols in many workplaces and, again, we emphasize that computer security has a long way to go.

MIS executives in charge of security have been pulling their hair out by the roots for years, developing ulcers, and occasionally becoming downright surly. It's a pressure job. But all of the problems in the past, within the last two to three years, have suddenly mushroomed by several orders of magnitude.

The personal computer has arrived, and it's here in the millions. Suddenly a corporation's or university's data processing is not longer confined to an easily protected mainframe; now it's spread all over half of Hades and the State of Georgia in LANs (Local Area Networks) and other dial-access systems. Every executive now, every department, every installation, every branch office—they all sport semiautonomous personal computers tied into the corporate or college network.

Computers are in more hands now then ever before. The Information Age has exploded on us before most people even realized there was one! And there's no going back.

Yet, most computer security people consider the personal computer to be their greatest headache and a significant threat to overall system integrity. Most people have computers on their credenzas now whether they need them or not—it's the status symbol of the this new age, a cybernetic "key to the executive washroom."

Any large company or other organization has constant personnel changes. Imagine the poor harried security person trying to keep up with issuing new passwords and deactivating the old ones. Often a window of opportunity exists for criminal endeavor. And, naturally, the greater number of people involved, the greater the chance there will be those who are careless with their passwords, or otherwise engage in improper security practices.

Networking

In a network environment you need to pay close attention to security. To understand why security can be so important you need to know the basics of how a network works. Here's a very simplified explanation offered by one of our guest experts, Barbara Hines—president of Software Services of Delaware, Inc. Barbara has installed more than 2500 network nodes, so she's very familiar with communications security requirements.

Networks consist of a server and workstations or nodes. The server is the main storage unit where all the shared data is stored. Each of the nodes or workstations is connected to the server via cables. When a workstation executes a program, it sends a signal to the server requesting data. The file server locates the information on the file server's hard drive and passes it back to the workstation. With several people accessing a single storage unit, you have multiple points of entry, similar to having several doors or windows on a vault. The more points of entry, the bigger the chance of unauthorized access.

You have to ask yourself what information is on my network and why would anyone want to access this information? In most businesses, networks may contain confidential information like client lists, purchase prices, employee records, and so on. This information might be the basis of your entire business. If this data were destroyed, how would your business be affected? In most cases, the reasons for tampering with a computer system are not to damage or destroy, but to steal. If one of your employees saw an opportunity to make some extra money by providing a competitor with a list of your customers, the effects could be devastating. And what if a disgruntled employee decides to get back at you for firing him and slips into the system? He could create bogus information or change his payroll earnings.

These types of occurrences have happened and could happen to you if you don't secure your network. What can you do? First, know and understand the security offered by your network operating system. Once you know what it can do, find out from the vendor what it doesn't do. Ask where the weaknesses are and what you can do to keep the system secure.

Look for the following:

1. Each user should have his or her own password. A global password for everyone is just a hair better than no password.
2. You want users to have the ability to assign security rights for each application on the network. This means one person may have rights to access payroll and make changes where everyone else on the network can't even access the directory. This narrows the potential of unauthorized access to confidential information.
3. Password lockout. If someone is trying to access your system, they may try to guess the password. With password lockout the person may make three attempts; if the correct password is not entered on the third attempt they get locked out.
4. When assigning passwords, remember that longer passwords are harder to guess than shorter ones. The rule of thumb is to use a minimum of five characters or numbers for a password. Try to use a combination of letters and numbers, for example your mother's initials with her date of birth.
5. Automatic password expiration. The more frequently you change passwords, the less chance of a password becoming known by several people. Every 90 days is a good time limit.
6. To circumvent unauthorized copying, you can use "diskless workstations." Diskless workstations are computers with no floppy or hard drives. If you don't have a floppy drive your data can't be copied.
7. If you have a modem on your network for remote access, you should have a communications program that offers a feature called *dial back*. With dial back, call the system to access the network. Key in your access code and the system acknowledges your call and then hangs up and calls you back. All this is done automatically, no user intervention required.

Probably one of the most important security measures is *backup*. Backups should be made daily, without fail. Our firm suggests a different set of backups for each day of the week, possibly by a different person each day. One set of backups should be kept off site. There are firms that specialize in security and will stop by daily to pick up a set of backups. If this isn't possible, have the person responsible for the backup take the copies home.

A disaster recovery plan is also one of the most important ways to insure your data. If you're working with a consultant you need to discuss such a plan.

Tailgating

Tailgating in telecommunications is exactly the same as it is out on the highway—someone following you too closely. The section above describes local area networks, but there are services called *packet* networks that tie computer users together worldwide. A packet service (the two largest are Telenet and Tymnet) have local numbers throughout the United States and abroad. The consumer computer networks such as CompuServe, Delphi, and the Source rely on these packet networks so customers can access them by making only a local call. But, many thousands of business also rely on these networks and can't afford leased lines and satellite up- and downlinks of their own.

Using a packet network is like riding the subway or a city bus. You can get mugged on the subway, and the same thing (though they don't like to talk about it) can happen on the packet networks.

The phreaker technique of tailgating is not new. It has been around for years, but more opportunities exist now because so many more people are "riding" the networks for fun and profit. Tailgating occurs when a session is abruptly terminated and the packet network computer allows another user to be patched directly into the first user's files, which are still open.

Even without malice of forethought (that is, a lurking phreaker) this event occurs reasonably often simply because the two major packets are now carrying millions of calls a day. System overload, a noisy line, and equipment malfunction are just three of the many reasons for an abrupt termination. On Delphi, users refer to it as "getting trashed" or "getting turfed." It's a common occurrence.

Users add to their vulnerability by getting disgusted when the networks are overloaded, so many disconnect without going through the proper log-off procedure. If you log off improperly, some phreaker may be running up *your* bill and enjoying himself immensely.

There are two ways to avoid tailgating. One way is to properly log off. The other lies with the packet network through engineering both software and hardware to make such unauthorized intrusions harder for the phreaker.

Hardware Security

Okay, most of the above has emphasized just how downright vulnerable computer communications is. In the next chapter we'll look at various *software* (program) solutions to the problem. These solutions include passwords and encryption. However, there are also hardware devices for enhancing communications security. According to a company or institution's resources, some devices that may be used are callback units, filter systems, encryption devices (as opposed to encrypting programs), and various unique identification devices and circuits.

Callback units do just what their name implies. When a user logs in and gives the proper username and password, he or she is disconnected. The host computer, using the callback unit, calls a prearranged number and connects with the user. The philosophy is obvious—even if a phreaker or other security violator hits on the right password combination, the callback will go not to him, but to the *authorized* phone number. A very real disadvantage of these units is that legitimate users can only call in from an authorized phone number. In today's wondrous world of laptops and other portable computers, this is no longer acceptable to many users.

While this type of device sounds like a great security system, it really isn't. As John Williams writes in *Computer Phreaking Addendum*, ". . . The only type of unauthorized user a callback unit will stop is some 15 year old kid with a C-64/ Vicmodem, and no mentor." He goes on to explain how phreakers can defeat callback units.

Filter systems are another way of determining that the caller is really a legitimate user. Filter systems are small computers between the host computer and the caller which demand a certain series of touchtones before access is granted. To the phreaker, this is just another computer to defeat.

Better than the two hardware methods above are unique IDs. These are circuits or other means of dictating times and locations that various accounts can log on to and from. They may be linked somewhat to a time lock on a bank vault. If a particular user account and password is only valid from 11 a.m. to close of business on the West Coast, no phreaker is going to be able to easily use that valid account number and password to break into the system at 3 a.m.

While a few of the more adroit hackers can eventually beat even this type of system, it takes them some time. And, if you'll recall our discussion in the chapter on physical security, the true purpose of security is not to make sure no one can get in (a truly impossible task) but to arrange things so the break-in is so difficult and takes so long, it's just not worth it to the perpetrator.

Mr. Williams, along with other security experts, recommends that the best communications security involves both an encryption system and a unique ID system. He stresses that this should be augmented with an alert and knowledgeable computer security officer.

Moving On

Such devices as those described above are out of the reach of many individual users, or those small businesses with local area networks. Yet, their need for security is just as the big corporations and institutions. And even the big guys should reinforce device-oriented communications security with software security.

That's what the next chapter is about—passwords, encryption, and other software-based methods of protecting your data.

10
ENCRYPTION AND PASSWORDS

Captain Midnight's Decoder Ring was a start, but the power of computers has lifted encrypting and decrypting many orders of magnitude higher.

In this chapter, we show how to use these techniques to protect sensitive data, and how to use levels of passwords to restrict access, or to allow it only in an area needed by that employee, client, or customer. The emphasis here is on the personal computer, whether as a stand-alone device or as part of a network. Basically, then, the methods of protecting data below use *software* (computer programs) as opposed to *hardware* (equipment).

Codes and Ciphers

The idea behind *encryption* is to translate text into a secret form that only a person (or computer) with the *key* as to how the file was coded can read it. The philosophy behind this is that no computer can really be secure. If a phreaker or ex-employee wants to get in badly enough, he or she will.

Once more (and this bears repeating), the basic concept of all security is not to prevent someone from breaking in, but to simply slow them down. You can't completely eliminate the risk of break-ins or theft—this is one of the few (if not the only) universal impossibilities. So the *best* any security system can do is to slow criminals enough that it isn't worth their time, or they get caught while still trying to get through your safeguards.

In implementing any security plan, from putting a padlock on your garage to protecting the Pentagon's ultra top secret computers, the prime consideration is "How much can I afford to slow them down?" The answer for small system or individual computer owners is "a lot more than you think." Encryption is an inexpensive way to drag the raping of your data down to molasses speed. Once thieves get by your password protection only to find unreadable files—necessitating perhaps hours of code breaking—think how very pleased they will be.

Encryption is nothing new, and predates computers by thousands of years. The Spartans, in ancient Greece, excelled in the military arts. Their secret messages were encrypted by winding a belt in a spiral around a stick. The communique was written on the belt and then unwound. At the receiving end, the belt was wound around a similar-sized stick, and the text was again legible. As Persian intelligence officers were wont to say of captured belts, "It's all Greek to me."

Julius Caesar employed a simple substitution cipher. In it, each letter was replaced with the one three positions to the right in the alphabet. Gabriel de Lavinde published the first manual on cryptography (the science of encryption) in 1379, and Sicco Simonetta wrote a treatise on how to break ciphers in 1474. Most of us have also read with fascination how the Imperial Japanese codes were broken during World War II, and the use of the Enigma Machine to unravel secret Nazi messages.

One of this book's authors worked with NATO codes in West Germany during his military service days, and deciphered encrypted messages in Vietnam during the 1960s. The incredible boost of information handling by computers in the last 20 years has also transformed the world of cryptology. For a few dollars, or even completely free via a free public domain program, *anyone* can have encryption abilities that make the best of NATO in 1967 look like *kid stuff*.

Encryption and *Your* Data

Information is valuable. Keeping it behind walls of security is a necessity in today's world. But, like bars of gold, it's not always locked in a dark, well-guarded bank vault. Sometimes it must be transported from place to place.

In the Information Age, the packet networks are the "Brinks trucks" of data transfer. However, through techniques such as that of tailgating discussed in the last chapter, the packet networks are essentially public. Even many intracorporate networks, whether the user realizes it or not, are really being transmitted on Tymnet or Telenet. After all, the packet networks make their profits by acting as a common carrier for telecommunications, just like a trucking company does physical freight. Even on a network in which the long distance lines are owned by that company and solely dedicated to just that one firm's use, they can still be tapped in a variety of ways.

Encryption, then, serves another purpose in addition to that of making a phreaker or other criminal's life harder should they try breaking into a system. It also *protects* data in transit.

One of the hardest methods of encryption to crack is called the *one-time pad.* Before computers, this consisted of two identical pads of paper, with varying amounts of text on each page. Two individuals or organizations wishing to correspond in a secure manner would each have a pad. They each agreed on a way to use the text on each page of the pad as a key, so the messages they wanted to exchange would be coded.

The person sending a message encrypted it using the top page of the pad, sent the message, and destroyed that page. The receiver took the top page of his pad, used it to decipher the message, and discarded that page. He then took the next page down, and used that as a key for the reply. And so on.

If only two parties were involved, this was an excellent way to send secure correspondence. Because there was no redundancy, anyone trying to break the code had a hard time analyzing it. However, for intelligence agents, carrying a one-time pad might have been too obvious, or they may have been unable to physically obtain a new pad. In such an event, the key could have been a certain page of a specific book. Carrying a copy of Mark Twain's *Tom Sawyer* across international boundaries was safer, or another copy could have been bought in case of loss.

While one-time pads are virtually impossible to break, they also depend on a very close congruence in size to the message being transmitted. For simple correspondence, this is fine, but for computer files that may run to several hundred kilobytes or even *megabytes*, one-time pad type keys are not practical.

One of the more common methods of encryption then is the same as the one Julius Caesar used—substitution. This can be done easily on a computer. In fact, coauthor Ralph Roberts in his article "A BASIC Program for Home Cryptography" (*Byte*, p. 432, April 1982) published a program that encrypts text files by simple substitution, except the substitution (determined by a key phrase) changes for *every line*. Even spaces appear as a different character in every line.

The article generated considerable mail at the time, including a letter from a university professor in East Germany. The program itself was recently reprinted in the book *Basic Programs for Chemical Engineers* (Dennis Wright, Van Nostrand Reinhold, 1986).

Yet, as many possibilities as this program has, and even with all the obfuscation of changing around spaces and word lengths, it's still just a substitution code. Those of us who like the scrambled word features in many daily newspapers, know it's possible to beat a substitution code with a little effort. A phreaker or other computer criminal, employing a computer of his or her own, can apply a *lot* of effort.

Your Bureau of Standards at Work

Quite a few of the encrypting programs available for personal computers today are far more advanced than any substitution cipher can ever be. Many of these now use the Data Encryption Standard (DES), published by the U.S. Government's National Bureau of Standards (a part of the Department of Commerce).

The National Bureau of Standards is an interesting outfit. It is the ultimate authority in this country for measurements. Exactly how long is an inch? The NBS is the *standard*. How heavy is a pound, or what volume is a gallon? The NBS is directed by law to be the final authority. It also runs services such as radio stations WWV and WWVH that provide the time, the *exact* time.

When the government decided an encryption standard was required, it naturally turned to the NBS to devise and maintain a standard (although the actual development was done by

IBM). The DES was published in 1977. It's an algorithm that allows text or object code to be encrypted using a 56-bit key. This size key translates to eight characters. If letters only are used, there are still over *200 billion* possible combinations. If numbers are used in combination with the letters, the possibilities rise to almost three trillion! Unless you're hiding nuclear secrets or Elvis' current address, this is pretty good protection.

This book is not meant to be a treatise on the complicated science of encryption, but only to give enough knowledge to wisely implement a workable and affordable security protocol on your system. So checking to see whether encryption software uses the DES standard before buying is all you really need to know. Since it's release in 1977, cryptologists agree that the only way to effectively break DES-encoded text is to try all the possible keys.

True, with the new supercomputers now coming, it's probable that some mega-multiprocessor monster will one day relatively soon be able to break DES, but few hackers or other ripoff artists are going to have these many million dollar machines. Besides, merely running the encrypted text through the program again *double encodes* it, and that would take an extremely long time for even a super computer to break. Even though it came out in 1977, the Data Encryption Standard will protect your valuable data for several years to come.

Let's look at two very reasonably priced examples of DES encryption on personal computers.

Incredible Power, Cheap!

DES techniques make for some very powerful software, and you can pay many hundreds of dollars for such a program. This might not be cost-effective in your security plan (and we'll look at security plans in the next chapter). However, there are a number of much less expensive alternatives.

One of these is the Private Line(tm) from Everett Enterprises (7855 Wintercress Lane, Springfield, VA 22152, 703-866-3914). This program is described in its accompanying documentation as a *shareware* PC/MS-DOS implementation of DES. Shareware is a computer program marketing concept which means you can get a copy of the program, try it, and payment is required only if you feel the program meets your needs. In the case of this excellent and slickly engineered package, the registration is only $30, and you'll be sent a typeset manual (the latest version as of this book's writing is 6.01).

The program may be found on electronic bulletin boards in many localities, where it may be downloaded to your computer free. Or, it's available through some consumer network services as CompuServe (in Data Library 6 of the IBM Applications SIG) or on Delphi (in the Writer's Software database of the Writers Group). On these services, you pay only normal connect charges. Another option is to order an evaluation copy directly from Everett Enterprises at the above address (in this case, the charge is $10).

Shareware is a great way of marketing. Support shareware authors by registering those programs you use on a continuing basis. This will encourage more great programs for a fraction of the cost more conventional software manufacturers charge.

The Private Line will encrypt any MS-DOS file (including *Lotus 1-2-3, dBase II/III, WordStar, WordPerfect, Display Write* and others) and will work on IBM PC/XT/AT, PS/2 and compatibles with MS-DOS 2.0 or later, including 3.0. The Private Line complies with the encryption requirements of the DES data encryption algorithm described above. Any file encrypted by either hardware or software which meets the requirements of National Bureau of Standards Special Publication 500-20, can be decrypted by the Private Line. It also supports the double encryption described in the preceding subsection of this chapter.

The fact that the encryption program you choose adheres to these *standards* is important. This means you can then exchange files with others who may be using a program published by a different software company, or who use another type of computer entirely. You can receive a data file over the phone lines that was encrypted on a mainframe computer, and still be able to decipher and use the information it contains.

The National Bureau of Standards specifies 171 tests to make sure an encryption program meets the DES mandates. The Private Line passes these tests (which are included in the distribution package so you can verify it for yourself).

Who needs the Private Line (or data encryption in general for that matter)? Here's how Surry P. Everett, developer of the program puts it:

"Anyone who transmits MS-DOS files of messages, data, or executable programs that are subject to be read, viewed, copied, or otherwise accessed by people other than the intended recipient.

"Users who communicate by bulletin board or other electronic systems such as Telex or EasyLink may wish to use the Private Line. Writers who submit articles over networks such as CompuServe or the Source should consider using the Private Line. Anyone who has sensitive data lying around on a disk should encrypt it in order to prevent unauthorized access. People who develop software in teams and communicate by leaving messages on networks should use the Private Line. People such as doctors and lawyers who keep personal financial records or other sensitive data on floppies or online, either on hard disks, bulletin boards, or otherwise, should use the Private Line.

"In short, anyone should use the Private Line who has something the user does not want to share, be it a message, a program, or just personal data."

For Just a Few Dollars More

Kinetic Software Corporation (240 Distillery Commons, Louisville, KY 40206-1990, 502-583-1679) provides another approach for $49.95, if purchased alone. The company just recently announced the addition of a program that provides government standard DES, as well as Kinetic's own proprietary encryption, to their other computer security products (which are covered later). It's called Kinetic Access Encryption Utility™.

The second, proprietary algorithm was designed to give a software encryption implementation that would be resistant to analysis, and would encrypt at a high rate of speed. Like DES, this is a key-dependent method. An advantage of this utility is that it can encrypt a whole subdirectory in seconds. Another option, which the company claims to be unique, is the ability to encrypt a disk completely on a sector-by-sector basis—giving even greater security.

Also, the user interface is designed to make the execution of either algorithm (DES or proprietary) simply by use of either a menu or command line options. All types of IBM and compatible computers, including the new PS/2 machines, can run the program.

Like the Private Line, Kinetic Software's Encryption Utility runs smoothly and quickly. It has the advantage of allowing you to exchange encrypted files with anyone else on the DES standard (and with whom you have also exchanged a "key"), and also to use the proprietary encrypting within your own organization.

Layered Passwords

Anyone with full access to your computer system can do anything you can do, and maybe more!

Encryption is fine for static protection of data, or to insure its inviolability during electronic transit. But what about operation of a system? The difference is between static and *dynamic* integrity of data. While a password (a "key") is useful in decrypting encoded data, it's even more useful to protect actual access to a secured computer system. After all, there's no need to encrypt data if someone can use the computer to randomly modify, destroy, or *find your key* within the system and decode data.

Some sort of password protection is necessary whether a number of people are using the same computer, or a network. Using different types of passwords (levels of access) with the appropriate software allows the security officer to restrict access to only what an employee needs to know in the performance of his or her job. An office manager can have access to payroll records, while temporary help or regular clerks will not be able to look at them.

If you have a computer at home, your children may be an excellent reason for passwording—especially since security software for PCs is inexpensive. Let them have access to games and education programs, put prevent them from getting into the directories that contain income tax information, home inventory, and so on. While your kids might very well be more computer literate than most adults, part of security is protecting from inadvertent erasure or modification of important data.

Earlier in this chapter we looked at Kinetic Software Corporation's file encryption utility. Their product, *Kinetic Access II,* serves as a good example (although by no means the only one) of layered-password implementation on IBM or compatible computers with a limited number of users (16). This program sells for $165, but does a lot for the money (as good software should). A slightly heftier version is $195, which includes an EPROM card for complete control of the boot process.

Both products offer 16 user levels that can be assigned by the system security officer on a hierarchical or individual basis. The officer can also assign Read Only, Write Only, or No Access for each user on any file or subdirectory. The flow of information to floppy drives, printers, and serial ports are restricted, thus providing "front-end" protection for most networks (stops unauthorized users, or those with low user levels, from making copies of data). As an added benefit, an electronic mail system is included so users can leave messages for one another.

This security system gives comprehensive audit trails on system usage and attempted violations. When running an application, *Kinetic Access* takes up only 7K of RAM. This is an important consideration on PCs which may be limited to only 640K).

A total of 16 users may be assigned (the security officer plus 15 others). Each user is assigned a user number, by which he or she is known on the system. Each user also has a password, which the person assigns to him- or herself and, at least under the best security compliance, keeps secret. To access the computer at all, a user must logon with the correct user number and password.

The security officer is responsible for maintaining the list of authorized users. This person can view a list of current users, deactivate users, or add new ones. There is an automatic timer, with the interval determined by the security officer, that will force users to change their passwords. Many systems have been broached simply because the same passwords were kept for years, and some of them fell into the wrong hands.

This is a good implementation of passwording in that not even the security officer knows an individual user's password. Individual passwords are maintained by the users themselves. The password information is stored in "an unconventional location" in an encrypted form. No one, not even the security officer, can know any user's password, unless that person divulges it or writes it down and tapes it under his or her desk. Such stupidity is still in daily practice, alas.

The security officer has access to the User Authorization Table. This lists the 16 available user numbers (the security officer is number 16) and their names. Each user number is a separate entity and can be granted or denied access to system features and menu items without regard to those of other users.

Using the Access Parameter Control screen, the security officer can structure *layered* access for each user. The parameters under control include absolute read/write. A sophisticated user, if not locked out of this privilege, could use a utility like Norton's that allows access to disks on a sector-by-sector basis, thus bypassing all security safeguards. Normally, only the security officer should have this kind of power.

Other parameters include preventing bootstrapping (resetting the computer), access to floppy drives and printers, disk operating system (DOS) access and, of course, access to various menus, directories and programs. System timer-control access is one of several features in *Kinetic Access* to help protect against computer viruses.

Such many-layered security may sound silly to the non-technical person and the security-illiterate. By this point in the book, however, we believe *you* are now a firm believer in computer security and the lengths to which it must be carried. *Kinetic Access* is a good system for the small installation to effect this.

For systems on which there are more users, you will need to look at software that provides for this. Later in the book, we'll have a number of capsule reviews to help you get started shopping.

Choosing a Password

In the last chapter, we talked about the "commonality" of passwords. We saw that many different users tend to use certain "popular" passwords because they're easy to remember. In choosing passwords, one must be much more careful. Here's a list of things many users base their passwords on which you should *avoid*:

• first and last names
• slang words
• common phrases
• inside jokes
• anniversaries
• age, height, weight, and so on
• license numbers
• historical dates, like 07-04-1776 or 12-07-1941
• your date of birth

Most of these you might choose can be pretty easily discovered or guessed by someone who wants to break into a system using your password. It's better to create a random collection of letters and numbers—the further from anything meaningful the better. There are a number of neat little public domain and shareware programs that will generate these for you. Coauthor Ralph Roberts' popular shareware program *ALIEN NAMES,* while designed as a utility originally for science fiction writers, offers a very flexible means of generating passwords. The program is available on most of the national computer networks, a wide variety of electronic bulletin boards, or direct from the author with a diskful of other utilities thrown in for $10 postage paid. (P.O. Box 8549, Asheville, NC 28814).

Here's an important tip! Most systems only ask for your password during the logon process. If you're on Delphi or CompuServe, or a company network, and the system asks for your password *again*, just enter some meaningless gibberish and let the phreaker bust his brains trying that one out. Whatever you do, *do not* enter a true password.

119

Conclusions

Encryption and passwords are both exceptionally useful weapons in the fight for computer security. Ciphers give you static protection of information, and passwords provide dynamic protection against access to the programs and keys that could break your encryption, or otherwise violate computer security.

Now, let's move on and take a look at how to plan *your* overall security protocol.

11
SECURITY
PLANNING

Any security plan, be it for a single home computer or 20,000 PCs spread around the world, must begin with awareness. It's almost impossible to develop security protocols or purchase security products without a pretty good idea of the dangers you're protecting against. So let's put some of the things together from previous chapters, and get you started on your own security plan.

If your neighborhood or the business campus where your offices are located has recently suffered a rash of burglaries, you will probably put locks or other physical security devices at the top of your list. If your computer routinely accesses "outside" programs, whether from bulletin boards or simply on floppy disks used by others, you *should* put an antivirus precaution as a line item on your list.

Using a couple of standard business school tools—risk assessment and cost/benefit analysis—anyone can come up with a weighted, workable plan. Since most larger business entities have an in-house flock of MBAs sharpening their pencils in addition to MIS staffers, let's lend a hand to the individual users and small businesses first.

Below are some of the parameters that should be factored into a workable security plan.

Physical Security

Evaluate the possibility of outright theft of your computers, printers, modems, and tape backup units.

A computer in a private home is an *unlikely* prize for a burglar when there are many smaller, more portable items around such as stereos, VCRs, jewelry, and the family silver. In an office location, consider the crime history of the site, if any (ask the local police—management agents probably won't tell you!).

Factor in those who have access to your office area—cleaning crews, repair personnel, painters, and so on, when your staff is not present. One "steal to order" computer theft ring in the Northeast operated successfully under the guise of painting contractors for a huge office plaza for over two years! And they weren't bad painters, either. Don't overlook the possibility of an employee who might "borrow" equipment.

Lock computer areas. This only costs the time it takes to do it.

Mark all physical equipment in an *obvious* fashion; "engraving" tools costs less than $10.

Cable components together and to a hasp fastened to a large and heavy object such as a desk. A contractor could probably do a tidy and workmanlike job using lightweight and flexible aircraft cable in less than one hour. Materials should not cost over $20.

Consider additional locks, either keyed or combination. In high-risk areas, consider alarm systems.

Data Security

Common sense costs only the time it takes to acquire and exercise it, so we'll look first at some very basic risks and the precautions that may be taken against them for *free:*

- Do not leave floppy disks out on desks where coffee or other substances might be spilled on them.
- Use disk banks with dust covers.
- Put floppies back in their sleeves.
- Throw away that magnetic paper clip dispenser.
- Make sure word processing personnel do not use copy holders with a magnetic bar.
- Label all floppies—both through DOS with the "LABEL" command and with a pressure-sensitive label. (It's a good idea for the labels to be the same. An unlabeled disk practically screams, "Format me!")
- ALWAYS take the time to do a directory of a supposed "new" disk. You may be surprised at what you'll find.

Now we'll begin to spend a little money on one of the *most basic* risks—loss of data through lack of an adequate backup. In the "big time" arena of security consulting to large corporations, this is known as "disaster recovery planning."

Purchase enough additional floppy disks to back up your entire system *twice*. Add good quality disk banks with *locks* to hold them. Begin the practice of frequently rotating backups. This is not the time to use bargain disks so you may spend up to $1 per floppy disk and $15 each for large disk banks. Be sure to store one backup far away from the workspace in a *safe* place.

Backing up can be "free" if time is not an issue and the DOS "BACKUP" command is used. If time is at a premium, or the tediousness of the DOS method leads to procrastination, spend the $100 (maximum) for a high-speed backup software package.

If several PCs are involved or if your data and time are mightily precious, purchase a streaming tape backup unit. A single unit can service several PCs fitted with the appropriate interface board. A single tape can usually hold the data from more than one PC and tapes are very easy to carry and store (for you *or* a thief).

Reliable tape units may be purchased in the $500 range. If you want to get really sophisticated, hire a hot-shot programmer to develop your own backup software to interface with the tape unit so nobody, but nobody, else can read and restore your data. Such programmers can often be found hanging around the computer labs of local high schools ($10/hour) or in the Yellow Pages under "Computer Consultants" (up to $200/hour).

The most valuable data backups should receive the additional protection of totally secure storage—a safety deposit box in a bank, in a climate controlled "vault," or a fireproof safe.

The authors do not consider any of these practices "optional" in security planning—the choice is limited to the backup and storage *methods*. The cost/benefit analysis is up to the individual.

Why the emphasis on backups? Because it's not a question of "if" one loses data—it's a question of WHEN. What's the greatest data thief of all? Your local power company and the PC's dependency on electricity.

If you don't own a surge suppressor, put this book down NOW and get one. (Maybe $50).

If you're located in an area where power is unpredictable, balance the value of your data against the cost of an UPS (Uninterrupted Power Supply) unit. And take a lesson from the pros whose lives depend on the words they write or the numbers they crunch—SAVE, SAVE, SAVE THAT DATA! Three hours of work on a *Lotus* spreadsheet can be wiped out in the blink of an eye. Three thousand carefully chosen words can be fried. Admittedly, as the authors know all too well, it's tough to "quit and save" when you're on a creative roll. Set your $20 computer watch to "go off" every 20 minutes. Then SAVE.

Don't overlook the tangle of cords and cables that spring Medusa-like from every PC. Find out where they go. OSHA (Occupational Safety Hazard Administration) rules do not apply at home. Jury-rigged connections, failure to use three-prong adapters, overloaded cube taps, a modem phone line running through a hall and across a work room are all accidents just waiting to happen—to your data and to *you*.

While you may get a charge out of personal computing, you don't want to return the favor to a PC loaded with data. Some antistatic device is indicated, especially in winter when central heat reduces humidity and increases static.

In an earlier chapter, we discussed the idea of thieves in three-piece suits. Change that idea slightly to reflect what *you* or *your employees* usually wear while computing—and call it the "Oh, $#@&" factor. *Everyone* makes mistakes—the idea is to mitigate the effect of what will, sooner or later, happen through inattention or carelessness. Of course, your current backup will be there if you need it—and maybe only a few minutes' or hours' work will be lost. But here are a few practical tips.

Practical Tips

Push the "off" button on your MONITOR (CRT) *before* you answer the telephone. This way you won't be tempted to continue working during periods of terminal hold or boredom.

Watch the screen and use the Enter and Esc keys judiciously. Too often, key sequences become conditioned reflexes and commands are performed at an almost automatic level. When we become accustomed to issuing a "print" command and hitting Enter three times to get things moving, the third Enter will be hit before we perceive the error message warning that continuing would be dangerous to our data. "Oh, $#@&!" Too late.

Be aware of keystroke differences among programs. Esc in one program may simply move the menu structure back one level—in another it may remove all new work and return the user to where he or she started—hours ago.

Read error messages—and think about them. A world-class programmer once lost a month's worth of work on a huge project (no current backup) when he failed to realize that the message he always saw, "XXXX.XXX already exists. Overwrite it?" was FINE when he was compiling new work—but DISASTROUS when he was windowing up *very old* work. Typing "Y" had become so automatic that his hand typed the "Y" before his brain has received the error message. (There is good news in such a situation—almost *everything* written a second time is superior to the first effort!)

Know the vagaries of applications programs and DOS. DOS cares not if a new file is created with the same name as an old one—the old one simply becomes history with no chance of recovery, even with the most sophisticated utilities. *WordPerfect,* the leading word processing package in late 1988, has the same disregard for existing work.

Don't overreact. Don't be afraid to seek help before it's too late. If all else fails, read the book. Uncontrolled keyboard mashing will almost always result in one or another form of disaster. From one end of the spectrum to the other, here are two stories:

First, here's the story of the executive who had recently installed a spreadsheet program on his new computer. He received help with layout, macros, everything *except* how to save his work. The spreadsheet—containing an entire year's worth of financial data laboriously typed in—was left "up" for almost 72 hours until he finally asked his 14-year-old son how to save it. He was too embarrassed to admit to the MIS trainers he hadn't "learned" this step. And he didn't read the book *or* call for help.

The second story involves the "power user" who was asked to learn, simultaneously, the protocols and procedures for three different "online" services because her management *required* such capability *immediately*. Mentally exhausted and completely confused by the service's different requirements as well as "under the gun" because the data was immediately required, the power user hit the keyboard with her fist in frustration. Keyboards are more durable than the human body. The user broke her little finger and painfully asked a calmer colleague to continue the project while she made her way to the emergency room of a local hospital. The power user was too tired and frustrated to call up the service's HELP function or to ask the calmer colleague for assistance *before* she was out of control.

The above are procedures and ideas, while based in very little more than old-fashioned clear thinking. But remember, most data is lost to either user error or power abnormalities.

Security Utilities

Moving into the area of more sophisticated (and expensive) security utilities, it's important to understand that there will probably be *many* vendors who have identified a "need," written software to meet it, and are aggressively marketing the product. Sometimes the promotional literature is written far better than the software!

The software selection process, like any other, begins with identifying needs. Large corporations usually use an "MDR" (Minimum Design Requirement) method. Smaller users tend to be more attracted by the bells and whistles. Know what you want the software to DO and the consequences if it DOESN'T. Start your research with one of the ubiquitous buyers' guides found in any bookstore.

If you or any of your colleagues have an extensive collection of computer magazines, check to see if the type of product you're seeking has been reviewed. (Don't overlook your local public library as a resource!) The research process will often alert you to additional features and ideas. Consult others who have similar needs. A simple question at your local users' group will almost always yield sound, practical advice from the experience of a wide variety of computerists.

Password Protection. Passwording is often indicated when several operators use a single PC. If the office manager and a data entry clerk share a machine, the payroll records should be available ONLY to the office manager. If the small business owner keeps all business records on a PC that's also used during times of "crunch" by temporary help hired from the outside, those records should be protected from unauthorized access.

Even home computers can sometimes benefit from passwording—to prevent the computer literate babysitter from spending a long evening telecommunicating with a pal in Hawaii, to keep Mom's personal journal safe from prying eyes and fingers, or just to stop the kids from playing computer games when they should be doing homework.

Passwording programs can require a password simply to start the PC with additional passwording to move into various data areas (subdirectories). Or the password requirement may be limited to "restricted areas" only. Many password schemes can be bypassed by simply booting the PC from a DOS floppy in the A: drive. Other approaches, particularly those that require the addition of a board inside the machine, can eat up precious work time while the system is "cooled out" after an operator's failed attempt to gain access.

Disk Optimization. The way DOS works, sooner or later your entire drive will consist of file segments written all over the place, not nestled cozily together. Disk accesses will be S-L-O-W and, if you wait long enough before taking action, the drive will just roll over and die. It's not unusual to find a 30 megabyte hard drive three-fourths full and running at ten percent efficiency.

Antivirus Detectors and Filters. If a "foreign" disk is *ever* accessed by a PC or if data is *ever* sent or received via telephone lines (modems), the PC is AT RISK, small though that risk may be. Every outside access increases the risk factor. These issues are covered extensively in *COMPUTE!'s Computer Viruses,* but there are several points that bear repeating (and repeating, and repeating).

Beware of virus-specific "search and destroy" software; it will be out of date before the programs can be compiled, much less delivered to you.

Do not be lulled into a false sense of security. Antivirus software should be considered as a tool in the larger issue of system security, not a panacea. Much of the responsibility rests with the user; regular and careful use of DOS disk management functions are essential.

Choose your antivirus software carefully for form as well as function. A program that constantly "beeps" or returns error messages during normal operations will become so intrusive that it will soon be discarded. A "virus finder" that requires extensive use of RAM may conflict with other RAM-intensive applications and the resulting "war" can leave the battlefield (your monitor) littered with unrecognizable high-order characters and no usable data inside the PC.

Select a "vet" utility (such as *Dr. Panda's Labtest*) that allows a long and hard look at new or otherwise unknown programs before accessing them through the operating system.

Software—for whatever purpose—has an obvious cost (the price tag) and hidden costs. The hidden costs include the time required to install the package and the time learning to use it. A "free" product that requires 20 hours to set up and understand is not at all *free*. Sometimes a product *just won't work*—it could be an operating system conflict (you're still using DOS 2.1? This was written for 3.3 or above!). Perhaps you've structured a PC configuration with so many "toys" that the program can't get where it needs to go, or maybe the vendor just sold you a bad product. The process of doping out what might have happened in such an instance can be a serious "hit" to anyone's time and overhead budgets.

Corporate Security

Huge volumes have been written about corporate computer security and an entire industry has developed around the issue. Many of the basic common-sense steps presented earlier in this chapter are applicable to larger installations. The problem becomes management's responsibility to train and educate users.

The National LAN Laboratory has issued a strong set of management guidelines and practices, endorsed by almost 70 different computer product manufacturers and vendors.

Their position document states: "Today's computer users require greater system reliability." If your business runs on computers, if your employees require computers to do their jobs, if you need computers to serve your customers properly, then reliable systems are critical to your business. Reliability is achieved by implementing several complementary strategies. The following is a set of industry guidelines for users; they are endorsed by the computer vendors.

Analysis and Planning—Every successful distributed system installation requires both site and risk analysis, and creation of a plan for disaster recovery. Analyses and plans must be reviewed periodically.

System and Administration—Every reliable distributed system should have an assigned administrator. The training needed by that administrator depends on the unique requirements of the distributed system and on the available resources.

There is a growing need for personnel trained in distributed systems and reliability. Vendors and users must support development of effective training programs to increase the number of trained personnel available in the future.

Power Quality Assurance—Many reliability problems stem from poor electrical power quality. Most of these problems can be prevented easily and economically. Distributed computer systems require clean, computer-grade power, free from transients, spikes, brownouts, and blackouts typical of commercial-grade power.

Servers, communications components, and critical workstations should have battery backup power and may benefit from intelligent power protection. All network components need conditioned power. The level of protection to be implemented depends on each organization's software and hardware reliability requirements.

Data Distaster Recovery Planning—Data backup and off-site storage should be an assigned task with continuing management supervision. Backup copies of all applications programs should be stored off-site, in both their original and user-configured versions. At a minimum, there should be an incremental daily backup of system data with complete backups of system disks performed at a frequency determined by the criticality of the data and applications.

The convenience of automated backup can pay off in added reliability. Established procedures for test and verification of backup data are also necessary.

Redundancy—All hardware and software components are subject to periodic failure. These failures can be the result of component deterioration, environmental conditions, or misuse. Some components are not critical to system operations and some can be easily replaced. But if a component's failure will cause unacceptable downtime, an identical, redundant component should be integrated into the system. This redundant component provides a system feature known as *fault tolerance,*— taking over and continuing normal operations in the event of a primary component failure.

Risk analysis will help determine the need for fault tolerance. Risk analysis also permits identification of particular system components where fault tolerance is a cost-effective reliability strategy.

For systems where downtime is not a critical issue, a policy for purchase and inventory of redundant components can provide cost-effective system reliability. Redundancy can be as simple as having tested spare runs of cable installed to be used in case of a wiring defect, or having a spare workstation, disk drive, or memory card available for installation in case of a component failure.

Management Tools—Reliable hardware components alone don't guarantee a reliable system. Equally necessary are software utilities to manage the hardware. Easy-to-use software tools for system management make local management easier for professionals and users and are absolutely necessary for remote management. These utilities monitor system health, provide warning of potential problems, and help managers locate problems quickly.

Systems that grow to include large subnetworks, or systems that are geographically dispersed, cannot be economically staffed with specialists at every site. Many important network management functions can be accomplished remotely with hardware and software tools. A systems approach using tools such as these can greatly enhance reliability.

Distributed System Management—The ease of installation and usability of distributed systems have been responsible for the rise of the myth that these dispersed systems, especially systems of PCs, do not need management. In fact, every system whose resources are shared by multiple users requires management. Computing is changing from several professionals managing a single computer to single professionals managing multiple computers in distributed environments. In these new environments, innovative management is essential.

A focus on system reliability is mandatory in today's computing environments. Reliable systems pay off in more effective use of resources, more efficient business operation, and more satisfied customers. System reliability in distributed environments requires a combination of hardware, software, and management commitment. **Note:** A complete list of the companies endorsing these guidelines is located at the end of this chapter.

The National LAN Laboratory states that the possibility of virus contamination can never be totally eliminated and that the level of protection should be weighed against the need and cost of the solution. The group recognizes that anticontamination measures will involve reducing users' access to systems and increased administrative costs.

They support a systems approach to reliability and give these specific recommendations. The authors' comments follow each recommendation.

All software should be purchased from known, reputable sources.

All purchased software should be in its original shrink-wrap or sealed disk containers when received. [There have been recent incidents where software in shrink-wrapped packages from well-known vendors contained a virus.]

Backup copies of all original software should be made as soon as the software package is opened. Backup copies should be stored off-site. [The ideal PC for making copies is the old-fashioned kind with two floppy drives—no hard drive. The machine should be turned OFF between copy operations and should ALWAYS be booted with an ORIGINAL DOS disk. New disks, freshly formatted, should be used for backups.]

Once purchased, all software should be reviewed carefully by a system manager before it's installed on a distributed system, or any system. ["Clean room" software tools that allow a look inside the software for telltale error messages, "Peace to all Computerists," are useful. "Stepping through" the program's operations with special attention to format and write commands at each menu level and choice will often spot a potential disaster.]

New software should be quarantined on an isolated computer. This testing will greatly reduce the risk of system virus contamination. Test runs should include a significant number of program accesses—a looping routine that simply accesses and closes the program is simple to create. [Test data should not include any sensitive information. The system date on the computer should be changed several times to dates far in the future as part of the evaluation process. If software is to be used on a network, it may also be prudent to set up a small model of the net for testing purposes.]

A backup copy of all system software and data should be made at least once a month, with the backup copy stored for at least one year before re-use. This will allow restoration of a system that has been contaminated by a "time-released" virus. A plan that included "grandfathered" rotation of backup copies will reduce risk even further. [Backup procedures will not reduce the *risk of contamination,* but will assist in recovery should disaster strike. Comparison of backups can assist in the detection effort.]

System administrators should restrict access to system program and data on a "need to use" basis. This isolates problems, protects critical applications, and facilitates problem diagnosis. [The hierarchy of security methods builds from physical security, to identification verification, to definition of user privilege, through encryption of stored or transmitted data. The highest form—audit—is absolutely dependent on the other four building blocks being in place.]

All programs on a system should be checked regularly for size changes. Any size deviations could be evidence of tampering or virus infiltration. Many good commercial utilities exist to perform this function. System files should also be checked as should changes in other structures.

Many "shareware" and "freeware" programs are invaluable applications. However, these programs are the prime entry point for system viruses. Skeptical review of such programs is prudent. Also, extended preliminary quarantine is essential before these programs are introduced on a distributed system. [Most corporations will require an agreement with the author of such programs before committing them to use, as opposed to the single user who may simply download a program from a bulletin board and begin to use it. Working directly with the author is the best defense.]

Any software that exhibits symptoms of possible virus contamination should be removed from general use immediately. System managers should develop plans for quick removal from service of all copies of a suspect program, and immediate backup of all related data. These plans should be known to all users, and tested and reviewed periodically. [By the time a destructive program makes its presence known, data may already have been altered or destroyed. The highest priority should be placed on the protection of data and its integrity. Managers should also be aware that the program under suspicion may also have created *additional* executable files.]

In addition to these excellent conceptual guidelines are other important considerations, many of which were covered in the chapter on "Corporate Initiatives for PC Data Security" in *COMPUTE!'s Computer Viruses.*

Human Resources Concerns

"Key" to corporate security practices are "management tools" and "human resources concerns" (words of the late 1980s). Management is responsible for policies, protocols, and procedures that will work equally well for users ranging from temporary word processors who view computers with some suspicion and distrust to "gurus" whose knowledge and skills are the stuff of legends and to whom computers are a natural extension of their state of being.

The development of security systems to span such diverse needs and abilities is an Hurculean task. The process of monitoring compliance may be almost impossible. Procedures that provide the highest level of security may be too costly to implement in terms of lost productivity.

When the risk from virus attack was first recognized, many managers quickly identified the greatest risk—"outside" computers and the exchange of information with them. The quick answer would seem to be a blanket restriction on imports, until the realization dawns that many valuable employees use home computers, putting in extra time and effort "without pay," to the company's great benefit.

Human error has been identified as the number one cause of data loss. It has become somewhat fashionable to point the accusing finger at users occupying the lower levels of technical competence and pay. If that's the case, additional initiatives for training and support are indicated. It is, however, far more likely that middle management employees lose more data than their clerks and secretaries. In most companies lower-level employees are *required* to complete certain training obligations and *welcome* the break from the ordinary. At most middle to upper management levels, a computer is a must, but training is optional. Training for executives *must* be action and results oriented, with the process taking second place to the benefits.

Those most prone to error in *any* situation are, however, those whose confidence in their own ability and experience is shaky. Add to this the proven reliability of the equipment and you have a false sense of security which, given human nature, leads to carelessness. Habit can become so strong that normal thinking processes are circumvented.

A new keyboard or a program upgrade using different keystroke combinations can also lead to confusion, if not disaster. Are there management tools to protect us from ourselves?

Any procedure should be evaluated for the human factor and it should not be underrated. In the good old days of the early 1970s when time and motion studies were the fad, an especially efficient operation was observed in a computer center. Operators would arrive at their workstations with coffee and newspapers in hand. Once seated, they would proceed to take on caffeine, read the headlines, and log into a monster mainframe without *once* looking at the VDT (monitors were called Video Display Terminals back then).

System messages such as, "WARNING! WARNING! DO NOT LOG IN!" would flash, unnoticed. Things have not changed. Just the other day, one of the authors, whose log-in to an online service is totally automatic, missed the "System Will Go Off-Line at 13:10" message at approximately 13:08 whilst grabbing a soda from the office refrigerator during the log-in process. Thirty furiously typed lines of information in response to an emergency call from a major newspaper were *lost*. As was the byline. By the time the problem was figured out, the story had been killed for lack of data and the newspaper's confidence in its "computer expert" somewhat shaken.

Just as "stupid" can be a problem, for whatever reason, so can "smart." MIS managers across the country agree that every company employs a cadre of computerists who are so technically superior that they are (a) essential to operations and (b) a continuing thorn in the side of management. These employees require special care and handling. Even the most loyal and devoted are likely to spend days, if not weeks, "playing" with new equipment or concepts.

The possibility of a sociopath within the corporate ranks is too unspeakable to be considered here, but responsible management *must* realize the possibility. The psychology of those who would spend most of their time interacting with machines rather than people, who would prefer to type "online" to others (in preference to using a telephone) must be a factor in any corporate security plan. These are the people who can "hack" either for or against you. These are the people who have the ability—and the knowledge that has been freely given to them—to do serious damage.

The extension of these experiences is clear to see: Any security system is only as good as the humans operating within it. Any security approach that does not include *people* in the *solution* and the recognition of *people* as the essential ingredient of the *problem* is doomed to failure.

The following companies endorse the management guidelines and practices of the National LAN Laboratory.

Advanced Digital Corp	Expandable Software
Advanced Digital Information Corp	Gateway Communications
Aldgridge Company	Gazelle Systems
Alloy	Harris Lanier
Alpha Technologies	Integrity Software
Alywa Computer Corp	LAN Group International
American Power Conversion	LANDA
Archive	Localnet Communications
Artisoft	Macola
Banyan	MicroSoft
Best Power Technology	NetLine
BIIC Data Networks	Network Compatibility Group
Blue Lance	Network General
Brightwork Development	Nortern Telcom
Business Works	Novell
California Software Products	Ontrack Computer Systems
Citizen America	Orchid Technology
Conetic Systems	Precision Standard Time
Connect Computer	Progress Software
Construction Data Control	Proteon
Convergent Technology	Quadram
Core International	Quarterdeck
Corvus Systems	Racet Computers
Datapoint	Salemake Sofware
DCA/10 Net	Standard Microsystems
Delta Technology International	SnyOptics Communications
DNA Networks	TDT Group
DSC-Nestar Systems	Torus Systems Limited
Easynet	Unisys
Elgar	Univation
Everex Systems	WordPerfect
Exebyte	

12
IBM PCs AND CLONES

There isn't room in this book (or any book weighing less than 500 pounds) to completely detail and review every security related program for IBM or compatible computers. Nor are we going to try. The programs and hardware listed below are meant only to be a sampling of what's available, and just a *starting point* for you.

Security programs fall into many categories—viral protection, encryption, passwording, backup, error protection, and more. Since computer virus protection programs are the newest category, and not yet listed in buying guides, we've placed the greatest emphasis on them here.

Use the preceding chapters in this book to help formulate your own security protocol, then find the software that meets your needs. Please remember that software is mentioned other places in this book, such as the Private Line and *Kinetic Access II* in the chapter on encryption and passwords.

DataLock

Product   *DataLock* Security System
Company   MicroDevelopment Corporation
           8 Milford Lane
           Melville, NY 11747
           (516) 673-9257
Type   Commercial
           $145

The *DataLock* Security Card provides password protected system entry plus device access locking on your PC system. Once the card is installed, it becomes an extension to your system's ROM-based BIOS. A lock is also provided to secure the PC case so the card cannot be removed. Because it's a hardware device that's automatically activated during the boot process, *DataLock* cannot not be circumvented. Software is also included, giving the system administrator the power to assign as many as 20 user IDs and passwords.

Each user ID has its own set of device access rights associated with it. Once logged in under a specific user ID/password, the user will only be able to access devices that he or she has been assigned access to by the system administrator. Devices that a user has been locked out of will appear as if they are not there.

The *DataLock* Security Card and the included case lock can easily be installed by anyone who has a screwdriver and knows how to open a PC case. The one we installed and tested worked smoothly and as advertised.

Data Physician

Product   *Data Physician* Software Protection System,
           including *VirAlert*
Company Digital Dispatch, Inc.
           1580 Rice Creek Road
           Minneapolis, MN 55432
           (800) 221-8091
           (612) 571-7400 (in Minnesota)
Type   Commercial
           $199

Data Physician is a set of programs designed to help protect your PC-DOS or MS-DOS computer system from software viruses and logic bombs.

Data Physician is a powerful, well-thought-out system with a lot of tools. The documentation is above average.

Disk Defender

Product | *Disk Defender*(tm)
Company | Director Technologies, Inc.
  | 906 University Place
  | Evanston, IL 60201
  | (312) 491-2334
Type | Commercial (hardware)
  | U.S. Patent #4,734,851
  | $240

"In the war on computer viruses, while everyone else is trying to perfect the bow and arrow, Director Technologies is manufacturing a tank! It's called *Disk Defender*."

As we discussed early in this book, the MS-DOS system of file management is very vulnerable. Viruses succeed, in most cases, simply because hard disks and floppies are wide open to infiltration and destruction. The *Disk Defender* system of plug-in card and external control box rectifies this design deficiency of all IBM and compatible computers.

The company also publishes the *Computer Virology* news-letter, offered free. Contact the above address for more information.

Disk Watcher

Product | *Disk Watcher*
Company | Raymond M. Glath
  | RG Software Systems
  | 2300 Computer Avenue
  | Willow Grove, PA 19090
  | (215) 659-5300
Type | Commercial
  | $99.95

Disk Watcher protects a system from viruses and also against "disasters"—that is, accidentally or carelessly losing valuable data, or just time and paper-wasting actions such as unintentionally hitting Shift-PrtSc. The program also protects against a full disk error message, accidental format of a hard disk, the printer not being ready, and the system date and time not being set (or the battery in the clock expiring). Numerous file and disk management tasks are also added, all for an expenditure of about 40K of RAM (the program is a TSR). *Disk Watcher* works on IBM PCs, ATs, PS/2s, and compatibles.

Dr. Panda

Product   *Dr. Panda Utilities*
Company   Pam Kane
           Panda Systems
           801 Wilson Road
           Wilmington, DE 19803
           (302) 764-4722
Type   Commercial
           $79.95

Panda Systems and their virus-fighting software have been featured on the front page of the *Wall Street Journal* (June 17, 1988) and in several of the major computer magazines. They offer the viral detection and protection package described below. Their system is one of the highest-rated for effectiveness.

The *Dr. Panda Utilities* detect virus, worm, and Trojan horse programs. *Dr. Panda* is a three-part software approach that should be used in conjunction with sound management practices.

Physical, the "virus detection" utility, compares essential system files and user selected files against a unique installation record. The system status is reported onscreen each time *Physical* is run. If a file has been changed, the filename is displayed onscreen. Any change in a system file, *.SYS, *.COM, *.EXE, *.OVL, or other program file may indicate a virus. *Physical* also reports the name and location of all hidden files on a disk at each operation.

Labtest displays the hidden ASCII strings of a selected file after reporting warning messages for calls bypassing DOS, or it writes to absolute disk sectors. Through the function key interface, the user may scroll through the file onscreen, perform basic editing functions, and direct output to a file or printer. Help screens assist in identifying and analyzing potentially destructive code.

Monitor automatically intercepts disk operation calls that request a format of any drive, or writes to the File Allocation Table of C: (or the first designated hard drive). The user may also select additional disk operations for checking (Read, Write, Verify) at installation. *Monitor* is particularly effective against Trojan horse programs that destroy data immediately as part of their operation.

The utilities provide a basic security system for PC/MS-DOS microcomputers. Viruses in computers, as in their users, come from contact.

Panda System's consulting and technical staff are available to assist in troubleshooting, advanced processes, and development of security policies and procedures.

Ficheck

Product   *Ficheck* 4.0
Company   Chuck Gilmore
                    Gilmore Systems
                    P.O. Box 3831
                    Beverly Hills, CA 90212-0831
                    Voice: (213) 275-8006 BBS: (213) 276-5263
Type   Shareware
                    $15 registration fee

Ficheck is one of several effective *shareware* virus protection programs. Don't let their low price scare you off; some of these programs are worth far more than the low registration fees. This one, for example, is but a mere $15.

In conjunction with the shareware and commercial products offered by Gilmore Systems, Chuck Gilmore also runs the VIP (Virus Info Palladium) computer bulletin board in Los Angeles ((213) 276-5263). You can call this board and download FICHECK4.ARC from the free area of the files menu regardless of whether you're a registered user of the BBS or not.

Both *Ficheck* and the VIP BBS are worth checking out. Chuck Gilmore and his Gilmore Systems have become respected names in the ongoing fight against computer viruses.

Flu—Shot+

Product   *Flu—Shot+* 1.4
Company Ross M. Greenberg
               Software Concepts Design
               594 Third Avenue
               New York, NY 10016
               BBS: (212)-889-6438 1200, 2400, N/8/1
Type   Shareware
               $10 registration fee

The original *Flu—Shot,* one of the first virus protection
programs, now has a new name: *Flu—Shot+*. Some "worm"
(as Ross Greenberg so aptly calls them) put out a program
called FLUSHOT4 which was a Trojan. Greenberg opted to
change the name.

"Besides," Greenberg said, "*Flu—Shot+* is the result of
some real effort on my part, instead of being a part-time quick
hack. I hope the effort shows."

Flu—Shot is now table driven. That table is in a file that's
named FLUSHOT.DAT. It exists in the root directory on your
C: drive. However, you can change its location to one of your
choice so a worm can't create a Trojan to modify that file.

This data file allows you to write- and/or read-protect entire classes of programs. This means you can write-protect from
damage all of your *.COM, *.EXE, *.BAT, and *.SYS files.
You can read-protect all of your *.BAT files so a nasty program
can't even determine what name you used for *Flu—Shot+*
when you invoked it.

Steve Gibson, writing in his "Tech Talk" column in
InfoWorld (May 9, 1988) calls *Flu—Shot+* one of "the two
most effective virus detection monitors available . . . ."

The right to use *Flu—Shot+*," Ross said, in explaining the
shareware concept under which his viral-protection product is
marketed, "is contingent upon you paying for the right to use
it. I ask for $10 as a registration fee. This entitles you to get the
next update shipped to you when available. And it allows you
to pay me, in part, for my labor in creating the entire *Flu—Shot*
series. I don't expect to get my normal consulting rate or to get
a return equal to that of other programs I've developed and sell

through more traditional channels. That's not my intent, or I would have made *Flu_Shot+* a commercial program and you'd be paying lots more money for it.

"Some people are uncomfortable with the shareware concept, or believe there's no such thing as Trojan or virus programs, and that a person who profits from the distribution of a program such as *Flu_Shot* must be in it for the money. I've created an alternative for these folks. I'll call it 'charityware.' You can also register *Flu_Shot+* by sending me a check for $10 made out to your favorite charity. Be sure to include a stamped and addressed envelope. I'll forward the money to the charity and register you fully."

Guard Card

Product   *Guard Card*™
Company NorthBank Corporation
               10811 North Bank Drive
               Richmond, VA 23333
               (804) 741-7591
Type   Commercial (hardware)
               $194

NorthBank takes a hardware approach to viral protection. Their *Guard Card* is a plug-in board that provides "true hardware-based write protection for your hard disk! It nails viruses and Trojans (and warts!) dead in their tracks."

The *Guard Card* prevents accidental erasures and formats when persons share a PC, such as in a networked system. It also protects turnkey user libraries from user error. The card supports one or two drives. One drive can be area-protected (requires partitioning). Works with any ST-506 controller. A system reset button is included.

Mace Vaccine

Product   *Mace Vaccine*
Company   Paul Mace
           Paul Mace Software
           499 Williamson Way
           Ashland, OR 97520
           (503) 488-0224
Type   Commercial
           $20

Paul Mace is an extremely respected name in the field of IBM and compatible software. The *Mace Utilities* (version 4.1, $99.00) is one of the leaders in hard-disk format recovery and maintenance. Their familiar ads featuring a Swiss Army knife appear in most major computer magazines. The *Mace Vaccine* antiviral package is currently being included free for purchasers of the *Mace Utilities*.

Mace Vaccine, says the company, is designed to warn you when unusual attempts are made to access vital disk areas and system files, not just by a computer flu or virus, but by any application that has no business modifying these vital areas of your disk. You can also raise the protection level to prevent any unauthorized access outside DOS. This will stop any of the current viruses "before they stop you."

Mace Vaccine is a resident program, and takes up approximately 4000 bytes (4K) of memory. It's most effective when placed first in your AUTOEXEC.BAT file. This is a solid effort from a solid company.

SoftSafe

Product   *SoftSafe*
Company   Software Directions, Inc.
           1572 Sussex Turnpike
           Randolph, NJ 07869
           (800) 346-7638
Type   Commercial
           $99

SoftSafe provides more than just virus protection; it's also a means of insuring data security for personal computers. This includes preventing unauthorized viewing, copying, modifying, or destruction of your valuable data, as well as offering powerful virus protection, according to the manufacturer, Software Directions, Inc (who also makes the printer control program, *PrintQ)*.

"The primary objective in *SoftSafe's* design is ease of use," said Geoffrey Wiener, president of Software Directions.

SoftSafe gives you password protection of your hard disk, allowing one "owner" to create up to seven authorized "users" for each PC. The owner can also delete users or change any password, and users can change their own password at any time.

Interruptions are no longer a problem when working with sensitive data. *SoftSafe's* lockout feature allows you to hit a hotkey sequence to cover the entire screen with the *SoftSafe* password display. Then, only *your* password unlocks the machine, protecting your data from unauthorized access. *SoftSafe* automatically encrypts data in designated subdirectories, so only the user who generated the file or the computer owner can access the files.

SoftSafe works on IBM PC XT/AT and 100 percent compatibles including the PS/2. The list price of $99 includes floppy disk and a manual, as well as 30 days free technical support.

Vaccine from FoundationWare

Product   *Vaccine*
Company   Mike Riemer
          FoundationWare
          2135 Renrock
          Cleveland, OH 44118
          (800) 722-8737
Type   Commercial
          $189

Vaccine from FoundationWare (as distinct from the similarly-named *Vaccine from World Wide Data* below, and several public domain programs of the same name) is sophisticated, top-end viral protection software. It's especially appropriate for networked computers. When *Vaccine* is installed on your hard disk, it continually tests files for the presence of any viruses, without the interruption of your computer's operation. If *Vaccine* detects a virus, it will prevent the virus from damaging your system while alerting you to the danger.

You probably don't want everyone and their "hacker brother" playing on your computers. If for no other reason, employees using software not approved by the company waste valuable corporate resources. *Vaccine* is designed to allow the system manager to control what software can exist and be used on a system, thus disallowing any unapproved software to run. This helps to standardize software and training within an organization and keeps people from playing games on your computers.

For additional usage control, *Vaccine* has a tracking feature that enables you to monitor what software has been run on your system and when. You can also install *Vaccine* to aid in determining the source of a virus (even if you approve an infected program).

Vaccine also reduces human error and recovers damaged or lost data. Again, this is sophisticated software. You may obtain additional information on it by calling the toll-free number listed above.

Vaccine From World Wide Data

Product   *Vaccine* 2.1
Company Ron Benvenisti
          World Wide Data Corporation
          17 Battery Place
          New York, NY 10004
          (212) 422-4100
Type   Commercial
          $79.95 ($25 site licensing)

Vaccine is a software viral protection package consisting of the *Vaccine* program, and two other utilities, *Antidote* and *Checkup*.

Antidote scans your disk for all viruses known to World Wide Data and notifies you if any of them appear to have attacked any of your programs. *Checkup* keeps a record of the state of your system, and informs you if any of your executable fields (*.EXE and *.COM) have been changed since the last time *Checkup* was run.

Vaccine is a resident program. Once you run it, you can continue to use your system as you normally do. *Vaccine* automatically and transparently checks every exceptional situation described above. If any program you run tries to alter your system in a suspicious way, *Vaccine* warns you about what the program is trying to do, and gives you the chance to stop the destructive operation.

Vaccine is a strong, well-programmed package already in wide use. It's well worth checking out for your own system.

Watchdog

Product   *Watchdog* PC Data Security
Company Fischer International Systems Corporation
             4073 Merchantile Avenue
             Naples, FL 33942
             (813) 643-1500
Type   Commercial
             $295.00

Watchdog is a comprehensive and sophisticated data security package. It offers ID and password control, multiple access permission levels, integrated access control, automatic data encryption, directory protection, audit trails, and protection against accidents. Fischer International also sells *Watchdog Armor,* which is a half-card hardware-augmented security addition for a system. The card provides a secure clock and the DES encryption standard on a chip, all for $149. Their most recent product is called *Mailsafe(*tm). This is a secure electronic mail system featuring encryption based on the patented RSA public key. *Mailsafe* sells for $250. All *Watchdog* products are available direct from the company or through dealers.

WPHD.COM

Product *WPHD* (Write-Protect Hard Disk)
Type   Unattributed Public Domain
         free—available in Delphi Writers Group,
         CompuServe IBMSW, and numerous other places.

This little gem will write- and format-protect your hard disks. Run once it protects; run it again and it unprotects.

Run this to write- and format-protect your hard disk. This is useful when letting someone else use your PC or when trying out new BBS software. Each time it's run it toggles the protection off or on—no need to reboot to get rid of it. The toggle ON/OFF feature will not work if, after running *WPHD*, you run another resident program that revectors INT 13. In other words, run *WPHD* after running other resident programs, such as *Sidekick*.

If the DOS FORMAT command is run when this is on, it will appear to be formatting your hard disk, but it's actually VERIFYing each sector, which does not harm the disk. Your data is actually lost during a format when DOS writes a new Directory and FAT—*WPHD* will prevent that. Actually, if *WPHD* is not installed and you accidentally start formatting your hard disk, you can press Ctrl-Break to stop the formatting. The Ctrl-Break will not be acknowledged right away, but that's all right—it will still break you out of format before any damage is done.

This one is *highly* recommended. Get it and use it; this is a lot of protection for *free*.

13
OS/2

Chuck Gilmore

Authors' note: This chapter was supplied by one of our several guest experts in the field of computer security. Chuck Gilmore, owner of Gilmore Systems in Los Angeles, specializes in viral protection and all aspects of IBM's new OS/2 operating system, including security. Gilmore Systems publishes the FICHECK *and* XFICHECK *virus protection software packages.*

OS/2 evolved not because of computer viruses and Trojan programs, but because of the higher computing demands of today's corporate and individual microcomputer users. This operating system steps away from the real mode environment of DOS and runs only in *protected mode.*

IBM PCs and XTs using Intel's 8088 and 8086 central processing units are unable to run OS/2 since their CPUs are only capable of operating in real mode. The Intel 80286, 80386, and 80386S CPUs found in ATs, IBM PS/2 models, and many IBM compatible clones, however, all operate in protected mode and therefore can run OS/2, which activates the protected mode feature of the those chips.

Fortunately, OS/2 solves many of the security problems associated with DOS. For instance, there are no interrupts (other than at the operating system level itself) that can be altered or changed by other programs. Instead, OS/2 uses *operating system calls.* In order for a program to get around those calls, it must have permission from the operating system itself.

In IBM PCs and compatibles, the interrupt table is stored at the beginning of memory, but OS/2 no longer allows programs access to the beginning of memory. In fact, programs can't get to any memory locations outside those allocated to them by OS/2 itself, and they can no longer trap keystrokes intended for other programs without first registering their intentions with OS/2.

Since OS/2 is a *multitasking* operating system running any number of programs concurrently, it must manage the system's resources for all programs. Therefore, unlike DOS, OS/2 allows no direct screen writes, no "clobbering" of operating system and other programs' routines, no more low-level disk writes, and no more "free for all" programs.

Programs can no longer read or write directly from memory. Even if that were possible, reading or writing directly from memory would have no effect—OS/2 swaps memory between disk and RAM, causing programs to think more memory exists than does—a concept known as *virtual storage.*

In actuality, it's easier to write a program for OS/2 than for DOS. For example, you don't have to write many different drivers for all the different possible display devices; OS/2 manages the resources for you.

But even with it's "protected mode" operating environment, in which programs no longer have free access to all of the machine, OS/2 still suffers in the file management area. OS/2's file structure is identical to that of DOS, so both systems can read and write the same files, and both systems can reside on the same disk, so programs can still have free access to most any *files* on disk.

Since files can be deleted, appended to, modified, and so on, Trojan and virus programs are still capable of destruction in the OS/2 system by damaging the individual files in it. For the tracking and checking of files, *XFICHECK* (described in Chapter 6) can be used for both OS/2 and DOS files. However, the program must still run under DOS (not in the DOS compatibility box under OS/2).

The DOS compatibility box poses another problem for OS/2: Although OS/2 is in charge, the DOS compatibility box operates in real mode, so running DOS programs in this manner negates some of the advantages offered by the protected mode of OS/2.

Even under OS/2, *device drivers*—a special category of programs—have access to privileged instructions and can do pretty much what they want. However, that shouldn't pose too much of a problem since you, the user, must install the device drivers and inform OS/2 about them.

14
MACINTOSH

The security considerations discussed throughout this book apply just as well to Apple's Macintosh computers as to any other. While there has not been as much security software available for the Mac (or software in general) as there is in the IBM world, more and more is beginning to make its appearance.

One nice thing about the Macintosh community is that it has responded with excellent shareware and freeware programs to fill commercial voids. One useful security program is actually *free.*

Secure

Secure is a program by Gary R. Voth (who may be contacted via his CompuServe ID of 72376,250). The program itself is available in Library 4 of the Macintosh Personal Productivity special interest group, and the only cost is whatever CompuServe charges for your connect time (use the key word "security" to find this and other Mac security-related programs). Mr. Voth grants the rights to copy and distribute *Secure* free of charge, provided it's not altered from its original state and is not sold for commercial profit.

"Secure," as Gary writes in the program documentation, "is a simple utility that lets you control access to your computer and hard disk. It displays a modal dialog box that prompts you to type a password and will not return control until the correct one is entered. By setting *Secure* to be your start-up application, you can prevent unauthorized users from booting your computer from any disk you install it on.

"As you enter your password, Secure displays the characters you type in an edit field. These characters are encrypted so no one peering over you shoulder can learn what your password is. A password can be up to 40 characters in length, and is case sensitive (upper- and lowercase letters are different)."

Secure, as Gary points out, is not foolproof. Someone can still boot your computer with a separate system disk, and he stresses that you should remember to lock your disk case. However, it will help prevent casual tampering in most typical business settings.

Mac Viruses

The Macintosh personal computer has been beset with viruses for at least the past two years. The "Scores" virus was first reported in 1987, and it's still out there and still causing trouble.

Viruses get into Macintosh systems disguised as stacks or applications. The virus spreads itself from machine to machine in this manner (being a self-replicating code). Viruses can (and do) infect such Macintosh resources as INITs and CODE. A "well-designed" virus infects other systems and attempts to hide code in as many "carriers" or Trojan horses as possible.

A virus, in the end, is eventually triggered and completes tasks (usually nefarious) planned by the twisted mind that created it. This can and does include numerous things up to and including erasing a disk on a specific date.

Computer viruses have an uncanny resemblance to biological viruses. In the Mac, they can spread from the carrier or Trojan (the stack or application that got it "through the door") into other places such as System files. Once entrenched, the replicated copies of the virus can lay dormant perhaps for days, weeks, months, or maybe even *years.*

If your Mac was infected last year, and you do nothing, you may not know it until next year. Next year, however, *boy* will you know it as files disappear.

A fuller description of Macintosh viruses and how to deal with them is included in *COMPUTE!'s Computer Viruses.*

Virus RX

Apple, like the other major players in the computer hardware and software business, remained markedly silent on the subject of viruses for a long time. Unlike the others, however, Apple did finally react to the pleas of their customers—especially after they were hit themselves with the Scores virus in at least their Washington office according to an AP report in 1988.

First, Apple called in the FBI. This writer talked to a couple of people who thought the perpetrator of the Scores virus would soon be brought to justice, but no one would say anything for publication. (Let's hope the slimebucket finds out that Justice is not blind after all.)

Secondly, Apple is providing a free program, *Virus RX,* along with guidelines on how to use it. This is, says Apple, "a public service." Survival is more like it.

Virus RX, according to the documentation Apple supplies with it, will list damaged applications, INIT, cdev and RDEV files, invisible files, altered system files, and altered applications. The program reports different levels of concern from simple comments to dangerous to fatal.

Damaged applications are the first to be listed. These have not been infected by the virus, but they will not work and should probably be removed from your disk. The program next lists all INIT, cdev, and RDEV files (such as the Easy Access, Mouse, or AppleShare files) in your System Folder. Many of these are common, but you should make sure you know why they're on your disks. Some files are normally invisible; *Virus RX* checks these and lists them. The documentation continues, explaining how to determine if you have a virus and how to remove the infection.

Virus RX is available free on Delphi, CompuServe, other networks, various computer bulletin boards, and through your local Apple dealer. It's designed primarily for the Scores virus.

Summary

The same security considerations apply on Macintoshes as they do on IBMs or Vaxes or Cray supercomputers. Generally these are physical security, data security, and communications security.

To boil this down, protect your Mac from being stolen by limited physical access to it. If it must be left unattended, the cabling and other suggestions in Chapter 4 should be implemented.

Data security may be gained through the use of such programs as *Secure* (described above), encryption, and by things as

155

simple as blanking the screen when you're away from the computer. This is the Information Age; knowledge is power and data is gold. Protect your information by always thinking security and using the basic procedures already covered.

Communications security has become one of the "big three" in overall computer security, thanks to the fact that millions of computers are now tied together via the phone lines. Even if you use your personal computer to do no more than call Delphi or CompuServe, or just a local computer bulletin board, communications security is important to you. Protect your computer from unauthorized access over the phone and protect your pocketbook by not letting your various system passwords get out.

Someone accessing a system in your name could do a lot of expensive and illegal damage. Let your password be divulged and the FBI might be knocking on *your* door; then you'll have to convince them it was a phreaker using your password.

Yes, think security and practice it. You certainly wouldn't want your wonderful Mac to become the rotten apple in the barrel.

15
STAND BY TO REPEL BOARDERS

"Those who do not learn from history are doomed to repeat it."

This quotation could have been written yesterday about computer security. The challenge to computer users and managers in the late 1980s is to dissect and analyze the wealth of newfound "history," separating fact from fiction, media hype from reality, and *acting* out of knowledge instead of fear or speculation.

Everyone is getting into the act. A recent editorial in the *New York Times* (Sunday, November 13, 1988) was entitled "How To Deter Computer Sabotage." The article had a pretty snappy headline and over 200 words of text, focusing mainly on the ARPANET invasion. The August *Times'* conclusion: Define electronic sabotage as a crime and *prosecute* offenders *vigorously*.

The long-standing definition of murder as a felony—and the existence of the death penalty in many states—has not seemed to be a particularly effective deterrent against the taking of another life. The psychology of the sociopath who murders may be surprisingly similar to that of the sociopath who kills data and systems. We are certain that this particular psychology will be explored at great length in days to come.

Crimoids

But the point is not *why*—or *what will happen* to the perpetrator. Just as we have learned common sense methods to keep ourselves out of harm's way (don't walk down dark alleys), we

157

must learn how to keep our data and our systems out of the way of those who would destroy them. Once one—or one's computer system—is dead or seriously wounded, it's too late to worry about whether a crime was committed and what the offender's ultimate punishment will be.

Donn Parker, one of the guiding lights of the security industry, is a senior management systems consultant with SRI International. Donn's brilliance and dry sense of humor led him to coin the term *crimoid*. A crimoid, says Donn, is "an elegant, intellectually interesting computer abuse method that receives extensive coverage in the news media for a short time. Some crimoids have caused relatively minor direct loss. All, however, have caused considerable indirect losses through the time spent by busy, valuable employees attempting to prevent occurrence of the crimoids."

Donn's theory, which is well supported in fact, is that intense reporting of "crimoids" seems unrelated to the frequency of incidents, depending more on how long public interest is sustained and on the priority of other news events.

He points out the two extreme camps of thinking about the current virus crimoid. One camp, beloved by the media and suspect among experts, features dire prognostications and the attitude that the four horsemen are riding at full speed with nothing to stop them. The second camp uses words like "prank" and believes the problem will fade as the public and the media tire of the issue—"Don't worry, they're only riding Shetland ponies."

The truth, as it usually is in life, probably lies somewhere in between. The optimists and the pessimists know no middle ground. But that's where most of us must operate. Workable approaches require recognition of a wide variety of possible actions. Parker offers some thoughtful, practical solutions:

- Patience, to give the news media and hacker culture sufficient time to lose interest in the latest crimoid.
- Increased awareness and motivation training for new computer users and for the population of future computer users.
- Vigorous enforcement of the current laws to visibly prosecute perpetrators as an example to others tempted to commit crimoids.

- The incorporation of features of the new antivirus programs into commercially available operating systems, where they would provide significant resistance to Trojan horses of all kinds (as well as many other integrity problems) yet remain transparent to users unless triggered.
- Greater quality assurance efforts among commercial and freeware software producers to identify Trojan horse problems.

Knowledge—Your Greatest Weapon

While we're taught that patience is a virtue well rewarded, today's fast-paced world of computing requires some immediate initiatives. The wheels of justice, to say nothing of the disks of huge software development companies, grind exceedingly slow. Two of Donn's excellent ideas are within the grasp of the individual or corporate manager: increased education and the selection of an antivirus software package meeting Parker's requirement of transparency, along with the "management tools" approach recommended by the National LAN Laboratory group (quoted earlier). *Knowledge is power.*

Ken Weiss, president and chief technical officer of Security Dynamics, Inc., a Boston-based consulting company, shares his theory on the "Six Enemies" of computer security.

Error, Ego, Enmity, Embezzlement, Extortion, and Espionage.

Error—This included the human variety as well as system "glitches" and has been covered extensively in this book. Nevertheless, "error" remains computer enemy number one. And good backups are the best defense.

Ego—The youngsters who became famous as "folk artists" for their graffiti in New York subways certainly have their counterparts in the computer industry. The original thrill of an undetected "hack" is quickly replaced by a competitive mentality, "I can hack better than you can!"

Enmity—Malice toward an employer or a competitor for wrongs, real or imagined, can be a powerful motivator.

Extortion—Imagine an employee failing to deliver backup tapes or disks to off-site storage and holding them hostage instead. Also imagine receiving a letter reading, "A virus is in your system. For $1,000,000 I will remove it."

Espionage—Ken presents three subsets to the Espionage Enemy—International Espionage, Corporate Espionage, and curiosity for fun and/or profit. The national and corporate issues are best left to those entities while we examine curiosity. Just as reading upside down is a useful skill in many situations, the ability to access computer data can often be fruitful or enlightening.

The possibilities for data loss and computer crime are, for all practical purposes, limited only by the ignorance and inaction of the possible victims pitted against the skills and motives of those who would victimize them—with or without malice aforethought.

During an interview with a national news network following the attack on ARPANET, one of the authors was encouraged to make a statement to the effect that the computer apocalypse had taken place or was near at hand. To the producer's dismay, the author put forth the concept that the ARPANET "hit" was the "end of the beginning" rather than the other way around.

Heightened awareness of security issues is long overdue. The media is quick to discuss the problem, but reporters are reporters, not computer scientists or security experts. Sensational problems are interesting—practical solutions are not. Even the best investigative reporter is limited by his or her resources and pressure of deadlines. The thoughtful user or manager has access to far better resources and tools.

There is an old song entitled, "Who Do I Turn To?" A Philadelphia radio personality, possessed of a classical education and a weird sense of humor, prefers to announce the title as, "To Whom Do I Turn?" Either way, the question is important as users and managers begin to evaluate computer security solutions.

Finding the Right Kind of Help

"Cui bono?" Aficionados of detective novels will immediately recognize this question as one of the most useful tools an investigator has. Its translation is, "Who benefits?" Keep it in mind as we look at another security situation.

A worried householder, victim of three burglaries, decided

to purchase an alarm system the day after the third break-in. Following the rules of careful consumerism, three companies were contacted—two "nationals" with full-page ads in the Yellow Pages, and a local concern that listed only its name and phone number.

The nattily-dressed salesmen for the two national companies arrived with glossy literature, mockups of windows and doors, and working sirens in hand. Their canned presentations were almost identical—with great emphasis on the *horrible* things that might happen to the homeowner, demonstration of the sirens, and their assurance of *complete* protection. Their prices—and the insistence that the homeowner's cats would have to be locked away while the alarm was armed—were almost identical as well.

The "local" was interviewed last. A pleasant-looking fellow, casually attired in jeans and a sweater, brought only a clipboard. He asked questions about the three break-ins, examined the physical layout of the house, and petted the cats who, in their catlike way, were curious about the visitor. The price quote was less than half that of the "big boys" and when he was asked about the cats, he responded, "A cat burglar is *much* larger than a cat." He was also quick to point out ways that alarm systems could be circumvented and the steps the homeowner could take to reduce those risks.

Transfer this homely experience to the world of computer security and ask again, *"Cui bono?"* There is much to learn. Any solution must *work* for the ultimate consumer. If a vendor's product requires significant changes in the way work is performed (putting the cats away), will the changes be so uncomfortable or onerous that the "alarm system" won't be used? If two products are essentially equal, are the glossy literature, audiovisual aids, salesmen's and managers commissions, and other overhead items necessary expenses? Very few automobile salesmen (who work on commission) could—or would—repair the cars they sell as part of the deal. *Cui bono*, indeed. Make sure it's *you!*

A bizarre twist to the issue of computer security is that the greatest store of knowledge is the property of those who stand to gain the most. To whom *should* you turn?

We should turn to the "trade press"—security issues are "hot" at this writing; books (such as this one) and magazines can be fine background resources. Pay more attention to factual articles than columnists' opinions.

Product reviews are the "Consumer Reports" of the industry. The popular computer magazines will likely print reviews of many new security products before this book appears in print. Several responsible third-party entities are also evaluating antivirus products. As one example, Jon David, a security consultant in Tappan, New York performed a study of antivirus products for Elsevier Advanced Technology Publications, publishers of the magazine *Computer & Security*. Initially, this report (to be bound as a separate volume) will be exclusively offered to subscribers of *Computers & Security*. It is anticipated that this scholarly report will also be offered to the general public.

The Software Publishers Association

The Software Publishers Association (SPA) is a nonprofit consortium composed of over 400 software developers. As part of its continuing educational function, they ask, "When a virus hits, who you gonna call? Virus Busters!"

SPA is very aware that the virus hysteria has made it difficult to find reliable and accurate sources for combating both the perceived and actual problems and addressing these issues in a positive way. To this end, SPA has formed a security special interest group (SIG) which we recommend as an important first stop for information.

The Security SIG provides a national and international network for information on general security issues. It also contributes information on viruses, a description and listing of "antivirus" products, and recommended policies and procedures to help curb the potential threat of viruses and other destructive code incursions.

The SPA is maintaining a library of educational and security related materials. In the future, the SPA will be promoting and subsidizing national and international security sessions. Currently, it's serving as an industry liaison for corporations, industry analysts, and consultants knowledgeable on virus and related security issues.

"The issues of security, especially the potential impact of viruses, cuts across all segments of our industry," stated Ken Wasch, executive director of the SPA. "The formation of this SIG provides an opportunity to establish a central and impartial contact point for corporations and press and software publishers who have questions and concerns regarding viruses."

The generally negative perception within the computer industry of "misguided" hackers and the perceived "profiteering" attitude of others is due to the misrepresentation by irresponsible developers of information on this very important security issue. Many industry representatives also feel that although the fear of viruses may be appropriate, responsible antivirus developers support the concept that their products are a management tool rather than a panacea. Several developers are serving as advisers to the SPA in this effort, including the following:

• FoundationWare of Cleveland, Ohio
• World Wide Data of New York, New York
• Software Concept Design of New York, New York
• Panda Systems of Wilmington, Delaware

Richard tenEyck, telecommunications director of the Boston Computer Society and owner of On Point Software (which does not produce an antiviral product) is especially concerned.

"The current hysteria," he said, "is disrupting the proper evaluation of the virus situation. Without belittling the potential threat of disaster, end-users and corporate security officers should able to contact appropriate and reliable sources for information."

The Software Publishers Association wishes to provide an objective forum for the exchange of information and ideas to address the growing security liabilities raised by the virus issue. The SPA is available for comments, and suggestions and can be reached at (202) 452-1600. Their address is 1101 Connecticut Avenue N.W., Washington, D.C. 20036.

The Computer Security Institute

The Computer Security Institute was established in 1974, and is a multiservice organization dedicated to helping its members safeguard their EDP (Electronic Data Processing) resources. CSI performs a major service by acting as a clearinghouse for computer security, putting members in touch with one another to share problems and solutions, keeping them informed, and enabling them to tap into the accumulated experience of practitioners who have made computer security work effectively in a wide range of organizations.

Members of CSI receive the newsletter *Computer Security*, the annual *Buyers Guide*, Hot Line telephone privileges, and reduced rates on other services and offerings. CSI publishes the twice-yearly *Computer Security Journal* and a 500-page *Computer Security Handbook*.

The $95 annual membership fee will provide you with an absolute wealth of information. An additional $140 ($150 to nonmembers) will purchase the *Handbook* and a subscription to the *Journal*. The $150 and the time it will take a manager to read through the *Handbook* will be time and money well spent. *Knowledge is power.*

CSI's headquarters are located at 360 Church Street, Northborough, MA 01532 (508) 393-2600. John C. O'Mara is the executive director.

User Groups

Users Groups are found throughout the country—almost anywhere there are computerists—and are one of the best places to gather information. Several of the larger groups (NYPC, for example) have had security special interest groups in place for some time. One of the great charms of membership in a users group is the opportunity to meet and share with others who "speak the same language."

Most groups provide question and answer sessions as part of their meeting format and you will almost always find several experts willing to share their experience and opinions. Many groups print lists of members willing to share their expertise in specialized areas with others. Both *Personal Computing* and *PC World* have recently published articles about users groups with contacts for those in larger cities. IBM will also provide a list of user groups to individuals upon request. Be alert for meeting notices on your local radio station or in the newspaper in smaller cities. Dues are nominal.

Security Consultants

Security consultants are popping up like mushrooms after a rain. Should you decide to seek the services of a professional in this burgeoning industry, choose with care. Many of the pitfalls that might be encountered are outlined in the chapter dealing with thieves in three-piece suits.

It's also important to remember that the industry is *very* new and the length of time a consultant has been in business may not be important in the selection process. Many firms that were early into the office automation game have changed their direction or branched out into the security field, often using the same personnel.

What does such a prospective consultant know about security other than the recognition that it's a money maker? A small young firm whose partners were data security experts for a large corporation before heeding the entrepreneurial call might be a better (and less expensive) bet. People *making* a reputation rather than *trading* on one, are often a good bet. It's experience *in security issues* that counts.

Check references for complaints. References should include satisfied clients and the Better Business Bureau. Most people know "somebody" who knows "somebody else"; the security industry is truly a small world. Make sure your proposed consultant is well respected by his or her peers and competitors. And think about second opinions. Two initial proposals are far cheaper (and provide much more information) than just one accepted and gone wrong.

The industry's worst task, one dreaded by all reputable consultants, is being engaged by a new client to clean up after a less-than-competent "colleague." The client's pocketbook and patience have been sorely tested and "consultant" has become a four-letter word. Such simple acts as reference checking, conferring with others whose businesses are similar, and reading the CSI's *Handbook* can help to eliminate mistakes.

Other Sources of Help

Don't overlook DOD ("Darned Old DOS"). Though sometimes clunky, arcane, and circuitous, your operating system can be a good friend. And, like all friendships, it *does* require understanding and patience. A lengthy listing of DOS procedures to implement against "nasties" is presented in *COMPUTE!'s Computer Viruses*.

Take advantage of your most important (and costly) resource—yourself and those who work with you. You should become part of the *solution*, not part of the *problem*.

Conclusion

"Do not go gentle into that good night . . . ." Dark though the computer landscape may seem, no one, whether an individual computer hobbyist or a manager of a huge corporation's information resources, is *alone*. This is the Information Age and an incredible wealth of resources is available for the asking.

"Ask, and ye shall receive." Just make sure your own good common sense is working as well.

INDEX

access
  structuring 59, 63
  to work areas 38–40
access code 5, 97
Access Parameter Control screen 118
Ahntholz, Ross C. 58
alarm systems 41
ALIEN NAMES 119
antistatic devices 124
Apple, and computer viruses 154
applications 154
attribute 31
AUTOEXEC.BAT 34, 47
backup 31, 36, 46–52, 105, 129–32
  archive 52
  incremental 51
  mirror-image 72
  rotating method of 49–50
  streaming tape 51–52, 72–73, 123
BACKUP.COM program 50
Baker, Richard V. 61
BIOS program 27
bit 29
Bleakney, Glenn 38
BOMSQAD 90
boot sector 33
bootstrapping 118
Boston Computer Society 163
bulletin board service (BBS) 69
  downloading from 79
byte 29, 31
cabling, hardware 42, 122
callback unit 107
capacitors 26
carriers 154
Chaos Computer Club 17
charityware 143
CHK4BOMB 90
CHKDSK.COM program 32, 46–47
classic penetration 101–102
clean room software 132
cluster 30
combination locks, use of 40–41
COMMAND.COM program 27, 34
communications security 2, 7–8, 95–108
CompuServe 106, 114
computer consultants 87
  choosing 83–91
Computer Control 64

computer crime 9–23
  and the law 4
  and the media 158
  and the trade press 21–22
  history of 9–10
  methods used 18–20
  prevention of 22–23
computer sales consultants 87
computer security
  and human resources 133–36
  enemies of 159–60
  in smaller offices 73–74
  methods of penetration 101–102
Computer Security Institute 164
computer virus 4, 20–22, 65, 67, 69–71,
    73, 75–82, 90, 98, 134, 162
  and Apple 154
  and conspiracy of silence 81
  birth of 79–80
  CHRISTMA.EXE 20, 76
  detectors and filters 127
  history of 76
  hysteria 163
  Marijuana 81
  National LAN Laboratory recom-
      mendations about 131–33
  Scores 154–55
COMPUTE!'s Computer Viruses 133,
    166
confidentiality, loss of 58, 60
CONFIG.SYS program 34
Consumertronics 15, 99
copyrights 91
corporate security 128–33
  management tools in 133
Craven, Sidney 44
Crime By Computer 10–11
*Criminal Justice Manual: Computer
    Crime* 18
crimoid 157–59
cross linking 32
data
  dangers to 55
  encryption of 63, 72, 109–116, 120
  inadvertent damage to 58, 60
data classification 96
Data Encryption Standard. *See* DES
Data Physician 138
data security 2, 7–8, 57–65, 122–23
  precautions 122

DataLock 137–38
David, Jon 162
DEL 32
Delphi 106, 114
demon dialers 100
DES 112–16
dial back 105
Diamondstone, Jan 88
DIR 27, 31
directory 27, 31–33
disabling computers 39
disaster recovery planning 123, 129
disk
    access 127
    floppy 26–30
    formatting 29–30
    hard 26–30
    operation of 28–30
disk banks 122–23
Disk Defender 139
Disk Operating System. *See* DOS
Disk Watcher 139
DOS 27, 30–33, 70, 125, 127, 166
    and OS/2 149
    compatibility box 150
DOS-level maintenance 36, 46–47
double encoding 113
DRAM 26
driver motor hole 28
Dr. Panda Utilities 140–41
dynamic RAM. *See* DRAM
eavesdropping, by radios 101
EDP (Electronic Data Processing) 164
encryption 109–116, 120
    devices 107–108
engraving 122
ERASE 32
espionage 160
Everett, Surry P. 115
extension 31
extortion 159
Fastback 48
Fastback Plus 50
FAT 30–33, 63, 70
fault tolerance 130
Ficheck 67, 141
file 30
    configuration 34
    deletion of 32
    structure of 30–33
File Allocation Table. *See* FAT
filename 31
file server 72
filter systems 107
floppy swap 33, 63
Flu_Shot+ 48, 91, 142–43
FORMAT 29

formatting disks 29–30
Forsberg, Chuck 95
fraud 58, 60
freeware. *See* public domain software
Gibson, Steve 142
Gilmore, Chuck 25, 67, 74, 141, 149–50
glitch 159
Greenberg, Ross 48, 91, 142
Guard Card 143
hacker 16–17
hard-coding 52
hardware 62
    cabling 42, 122
    damage to 58, 60
    marking 41
    security 42–44, 46, 71–72, 107–108
hardwiring 73
Heinlein, Robert A. 98
Highland, Harold J. 93
Hines, Barbara 104
Hopkins, Andy 26, 90
IBM 50
    security information 25–36
    security programs 137–48
IBMBIO.COM program 30–31, 33–34
IBMDOS.COM program 27, 33–34
IBMIO.COM program 27
identification, devices 107–108
index hole 28–29
industry standards 90–91
information theft, ramifications of 2–3
intelligence gathering 101
interrupts 70
interrupt table 149
IO.SY program 30
Jobs, Steve 20
key switch, use of 73
killer codes, protecting from 63
Kinetic Access Encryption Utility
    115–16
Kinetic Access II 117–18
LAN 103
Local Area Networks. *See* LAN
logic bombs 18–19
log-off procedure 106
Mace Vaccine 144
Macintosh, security programs 153–55
mainframe computer systems 61
    security of 67–69
Manager Information Systems. *See* MIS
Martinott, Robert T. 58
McCown, Davis 4
MDR (Minimum Design Requirement)
    126
memory 26
    and OS/2 150
MIS 57

Mitchell, Gerald E. 17
modem carrier 100
MS-DOS 30
National Bureau of Standards 112
National LAN Laboratory guidelines
   129–31, 136, 159
networking 104–106
node 104
Norton's Wipedisk 72–73
one-time pad 111–12
operating system, bypassing 70
operating system calls 149
OS/2 operating system 149–51
   and computer viruses 150
   and memory 150
   device drivers 151
   file structure 150
packet network 106, 111
parallel port 73
Parker, Donn B. 10–11, 158
password 5, 63, 72–73, 96–99, 102, 105,
   120
   automatic expiration 105
   choosing 119
   layered 116–18
   lockout 105
   protection 52, 127
   use in mainframe systems 667
phreaking 14–17, 97, 99–100, 102
   Van Eyk 101
physical security 2, 7–8, 37–55, 121–22
PIN (Personal Identification Numbers)
   96
POST (Power On Self Test) 34
Private Line 113–14, 116
programs
   antivirus 128, 159
   CHKDSK.COM 32, 46–47
   COMMAND.COM 27, 34
   CONFIG.SYS 34
   custom 87, 89
   executive 62
   IBMBIO.COM 30–31, 33–34
   IBMDOS.COM 27, 33–34
   IBMIO.COM 27
   install 35
   IO.SY 30
   off-the-shelf 87, 89
   RESTORE 50
   system 33–35
   trap door 18–20
   Trojan horse 4, 20, 67, 69–70, 72, 90,
      154, 159
   TSR 6, 63, 70–71
protected mode 149–50
public domain software 62, 90–91,
   113–14, 133, 153

RAM 6, 26, 63
   scrambling by power browns 26
RamNet 48
Random Access Memory. *See* RAM
raw code 93
Read-Only Memory. *See* ROM
read/write head 28–29
real mode 69–70, 149
recovery, of data 64
RESTORE program 50
risk analysis 129–30
ROM 30–31, 34
round down technique 19
Rubin, Diana 45
salami technique 19
screen prompts 27
sector 29–32
Secure 153
security
   consultants 165
   planning 121–36
   utilities 126–28
Security Special Interest Group (SIG)
   162
serial port 73
server 104
service calls. *See* SVC
service contracts 88
servicing, of computers 63
shareware. *See* public domain software
side 29
SideKick Plus 70
sigma 32
social engineering 100
SoftSafe 144–45
software 62
   "miracle" 6
   copyrights to 91
   pirated 89–90
   protection of data 62–64
Software Publishers Association (SPA)
   162–63
Source, The 106
stacks 154
stepping through programs 132
Stoll, Clifford 97–98
storage, of data 123, 129
substitution code 112
superzapping 19
surge suppressor 52, 124
SVC 69
tailgaiting 106–107, 111
tampering 58, 60
Telenet 106, 111
telephones, and computer security
   95–97, 100
televaulting 45

tempest methods of penetration 101–102
tenEyck, Richard 163
Terminate and Stay Resident utility. *See* TSR
track 29
triple barrier protection 23
TSR program 6, 63, 70–71
  virus blockers 70
Tymnet 106, 111
Uninterrupted Power Supply system. *See* UPS system
UPS system 52, 124
User Authorization Table 118
user groups 164–65
usernames 96
Vaccine from FoundationWare 145–46
Vaccine from World Wide Data 146–47
VAD (Value-Added Dealer) 88
Value-Added Dealer. *See* VAD
Value-Added Retailer. *See* VAR
van Eyk, Wim 101–102
vaporware 7

VAR (Value-Added Retailer) 88
vaults, use of 44–45
vet utility 128
VIP (Virus Info Palladium) 141
virtual format 80
virtual storage 150
Virus RX 154–55
Voth, Gary R. 153
wargame dialers 100
Wasch, Ken 163
Watchdog 147
Weiss, Ken 159
Williams, John J. 15, 99, 101, 107–108
Winton, John M. 58
wiretapping 101
workstation 104
  diskless 105
worm 4, 98
WPHD.COM program 28, 148
WriteGuard 33
write-protect notch 28
XFICHECK 67, 71, 150

COMPUTE! Books

Ask your retailer for these **COMPUTE! Books** or order directly from
COMPUTE!.

Call toll free (in US) **1-800-345-1214** (in PA 215-964-4000) or write COM-
PUTE! Books, P.O. Box 2165, Radnor, PA 19089.

Quantity	Title	Price*	Total
_____	COMPUTE!'s Using Borland's *Sprint* (C1420)	**$17.95**	_____
_____	COMPUTE!'s Buyer's Guide to IBM PCs, Compatibles, and Portables (C1234)	**$12.95**	_____
_____	Hard Disk Management (C1161)	**$19.95**	_____
_____	PC/MS-DOS Made Easy (C1382)	**$15.95**	_____
_____	*PC-Write* Simplified (C1250)	**$16.95**	_____
_____	COMPUTE!'s Mastering *MultiMate Advantage II* (C1544)	**$19.95**	_____
_____	COMPUTE!'s Mastering PC *Works* (C1390)	**$19.95**	_____
_____	COMPUTE!'s Using *Microsoft Excel* on the IBM (C1471)	**$21.95**	_____
_____	COMPUTE!'s Computer Viruses (C1781)	**$14.95**	_____

*Add $2.50 for first book, $.50 each additional book for shipping and handling.
Outside US add $5.00.

PA residents add 6% sales tax _____

Shipping & handling _____

Total payment _____

All orders must be prepaid (check, charge, or money order).
All payments must be in US funds.
☐ Payment enclosed.
Charge   ☐ Visa   ☐ MasterCard

Acct. No._____ Exp. Date_____
(Required)

Signature_____

Name_____

Address_____

City_____ State _____ Zip_____

*Allow 4–5 weeks for delivery.
Prices and availability subject to change.
Current catalog available upon request.